Music Saved My Life
From Darkness Into The Light

My Life As A 70's R&B/Soul Singer

BY
OLLAN CHRISTOPHER BELL
(aka Chris James)

Published by: Boogie With The Hook Inc.

All characters in this book are real and true events are depicted.

The cataloging-in-publication data is on file with the Library of Congress.

Library of Congress Control Number: 1-5720374587

ISBN: 978-0-9987950-0-3

Copyright © 2017 by Ollan Christopher Bell

Printed in the United States of America

Printed in 2017

Genre: Non-Fiction/Autobiography

DEDICATION

This book is dedicated to my brother Joseph Diamond Bell (1947-2015) and his two beautiful daughters Monique Antoinette Payton and Paulina Sabrina Joelle Bell. (Paulina, we are still searching for you and hope to find you one day.)

This book is also dedicated to all the fans, past and present, who have loved and supported the music of the Natural Four.

CONTENTS

Preface

"The Natural Four sang some of the sweetest harmonies ever recorded. They (TN4) deserved more acclaim, as they had a crisp, smooth, lead singer in Chris James."

Lonnie Cook, songwriter,
"I Thought You Were Mine," our first single

Music Saved My Life
From Darkness Into The Light

My Life as a 70's R/B/Soul Singer

Now that you have purchased your ticket, you will be escorted to the front row seat of your desired location. Once you are seated comfortably, with your favorite snack and beverage, indulge your mind in this sensational story. Enjoy!

Christopher James

1
The Beginning

I was born on Tuesday, June 15, 1943, in Oakland California, and given the name Ollan Christopher Bell by my mother, Earline Odell Jordan. My mother, also known as *Arvanola* by some and *Toots* by close friends, came from a family of Black achievers. My grandparents stressed education, encouraging my mother and her sisters to pursue professional careers at a time when blacks in higher education were still a novelty. Neither my grandmother nor my grandfather could read very well, but both knew that without a good education life would be very difficult.

My two aunts, Tillie and Stella Jordan, took this advice to heart. Both pursued higher education. Aunt Tillie even served as a principal in the Los Angeles school district for many years. Mother was just as articulate as my aunts, but she wanted to pursue a career in the entertainment business but, of course, my grandmother and grandfather were against it.

The youngest of the three Jordan girls, Papa treated young *Arvanola* like the boy he so desperately wanted to have. A rumor circulated that my mother was not really my grandfather's daughter. As always, it was difficult to determine the truth where Mother was concerned.

Mother was an imposing woman who stood five feet and nine and a half inches tall. With her medium brown complexion and big-boned figure, she had all the required features to be called a "fox." Her hair was thick and full. Her pretty face, beauty, and great vocal talent gave her what it took to make it as a singer, yet Mother's dream of a career in the spotlight was quickly derailed after the birth of my oldest sister, Lynne, to a man named Peter Du Heart. I don't remember much about him other than a few appearances when I was very young. Mother was what we call today a *player*. Aside from assumptions, I cannot talk much about her life because Mother was very secretive. We were told what she wanted us to know, which was very little.

From all the information I have been given, remarks made by my mother and grandmother, I was the result of a one-night stand with a man by the name of Paul Reeves Johnson, reputedly of Ethiopian extraction. I am not certain of anything about my biological father. The only circumstantial clue I ever had concerning my paternal lineage came many years later when I was on a trip to Amsterdam, and a group of Ethiopians approached me speaking in their native language. I guessed they thought I was Ethiopian. Aside from casual remarks from friends and acquaintances suggesting I could pass for Ethiopian, I had little in the way of hard evidence to confirm or deny this heritage. In any case, the result was, and is to this day, that I am a person like many others, who will go to his grave not knowing his father.

Paul Reeves Johnson (my father, according to my mother)

For legal purposes, my paternity was attributed to Christopher Bell, my mother's husband at the time, and father of my brother Joseph and sister Rosie. Chris was a good man, but he married my mother twice. I never could understand that. He was the only real father figure that I ever had, even though half the time he wasn't around because he was a long distance truck driver. And even though he knew that I was not his son he always treated me as if I were. Mother had three more children; their names are Albert

Parry, Caesar Jr. (who has since passed), and Keola Wayne, by a man who was strange to me at the time, but I was not sure what it was. Back then the concept of homosexuality was not talked about. It was taboo, although I knew something was different about this person.

Mother was controlling, possessive, and secretive, which made her an extremely formidable woman with a certain mystique. She used these qualities to exert a high level of influence on many of my most important life decisions. She came from the old school, which meant discipline consisted of extension cords and tree switches. As abhorrent as corporal punishment is today, it was squarely within the norm of that era, especially among African American families. Despite her strong disciplinary style, she was very affectionate and attentive, to a degree. Mother always told us how much she loved us, to which I would ask, "Why do you whip us if you love us?" And I'd get my ass beat again.

Mother was also believed to have a gift of mystical sorts. These powers brought people from all over Oakland to our home for readings and séances. One of her students in spirituality was Jim Jones, who would later become infamous for his central role in the Jonestown, Guyana, mass suicide tragedy in 1978.

I spent most of my formative years in Oakland, at that time a predominantly white city. We moved around a lot in the Oakland Bay Area, my mother would move with the four of us older children, from East Oakland to West Oakland, to live with my grandfather or grandmother, depending on who she was on good terms with at the time. The two main family residences where we spent our childhood were 8801 A Street and 819 Center Street, both still standing. My grandmother and grandfather got divorced long before I was born, but Papa still visited my grandmother from time to time, and took us to the park, the San Francisco Zoo, and to the merry-go-round by the water. Papa was a big man over six feet tall and soft-spoken, at least with us. Papa never said much for the most part; he was a quiet man. I don't remember much about him except that he had us over to his house on Center Street where we would watch TV until the channels went off the air, and Papa fell asleep. Back then, to be Black and own a TV was a big deal. Papa worked for Southern

Pacific Railroad as a mail handler, so he frequently traveled in and out of town. Papa was a hard worker and that is where I developed my work ethic.

In the late 1940s and 1950s it was common to see all kinds of animals in Oakland. We had our share of domesticated animals: we raised chickens, rabbits, ducks, pigeons, turkeys, and one goat. We planted gardens, picked fruit, and took care of the livestock. We had another house on 85th Avenue, one of the many homes my grandfather owned, where we spent a lot of time in our later years. Papa always bought us a dog, and I remember him getting me my first dog.

When we lived on 85th Avenue we owned a lot of chickens that we had to feed and clean up after. I could be exaggerating but there seemed to be at least 100 of them. We also had a lot of fruit trees: apple, plum, cherry, orange, and pear. But we spent most of the time taking care of the nasty chickens. I guess it was part of our training. We used to do bad things to the chickens, like put their heads in water and play like we were on horseback with a stick and run past the chickens, whacking at their heads. We never killed any of them, but when I look back, it wasn't a nice thing to do to them.

We spent most of our time at home because we were told it was the best place for us. Oakland was a very nice city in those days. There was not much crime, education was at the forefront of the city's priorities, and the it was populated with a mix of ethnicities that got along together well. There were a lot of Italians, a large population of Germans, and a few Asians. Most of all, we had a lot of white American people. My two best friends were white; their names were James O'Neal and Tommy Bolin. I never went to their homes so I guess they were not my best friends after all. I had two black friends, Steven Harris and Bobby Keys, along with several Hispanic friends.

Life was very quiet for us. I never heard the word *nigger* used other than in my home, and then not often. The grammar school I attended was mostly white but I was never called a *nigger* there. I do remember being bullied by some black guys at the school. My siblings and I wore clothes handed down to us from some of the white kids who attended school with us. Every year, usually around Christmas, schoolmates would leave old clothes on our front porch at the A Street House. It was rough sometimes, because the other kids would make fun of me. So, I learned early on to swallow my tears and pretend it was nothing. But it hurt very much, and I would cry when alone. It was a strange thing; Mother had the money to buy us new clothes but, for some reason, she would never spend it, at least not on us.

There were many men who came and went in our lives. Mother was married several times, twice to Christopher Bell, as I mentioned earlier, and she had many other men between marriages. She married her last husband, Caesar James, when I was nine or ten years old. This was a marriage based on money and convenience, from the start. I vividly recall the day when Caesar, about six foot one and nearly 225 pounds, and his family drove in from a tobacco farm in Virginia carrying a pot-bellied stove full of silver dollars to sweeten the marriage deal. I wasn't impressed with this man from the first day I saw him. I knew there was something wrong. It was in the morning, and some people came to the house on A Street, sat around the table and talked for a while. They stayed for about two days, and then his family went back to Virginia and Caesar remained at our house. Later on in life I understood what I was feeling about him.

Homosexuality was not a concept that resonated in my young mind at the time. Caesar was simply different. He was an excellent singer and great cook. He was also quite fastidious when it came to his appearance and household cleanliness. He wasn't into the typical "man thing" at all. Caesar's effeminate voice starkly contrasted with his burly stature, and he always smelled of Magic Shave, a popular beard removal powder of the era that I would come to use as an adult. Consistent with antiquated notions that homosexuality was a curable condition, Mama and Mother were intent upon making Caesar James a man. Mother's frequent attempts to seduce her new husband were met with rejection. When they would be in the front bedroom at the house on A Street, Mother would be all over him, not thinking about us kids, making him laugh and talking to him. She

12

tried to make him have sex with her. I guess you could say Mother's behavior was a crude form of conversion therapy. Her attempts were to no avail. Even I could see, at a young age, that Mother's offers of consummating the marriage were just not his thing. Caesar eventually gave in and my half-brother Albert was born.

Despite the infrequency of marital sex, Caesar managed to integrate himself into the household almost immediately. The relationship between Mother and Caesar often resembled that of a mother and son. Caesar was barely literate, so it was hard for him to find a job because he could not pass the written test. Mother encouraged Caesar to overcome his illiteracy and nurtured him in other pursuits. She even secured a job for him at Children's Hospital in Oakland. He worked there for almost fifteen years. In contrast to his antagonistic feelings for me, Caesar loved both of my sisters, Lynne and Rose, sharing an especially deep bond with Lynne.

Lynne was a very beautiful girl who liked to dress up and paint her nails, you know, the things that most young ladies do. Caesar would always help her with her hair and nails. One particular evening, when Mother and Caesar were about a year or so into their marriage, we had the kerosene heaters going in the front room - it was real cold outside. Lynne was standing in front of the heater. We were told never to get too close because of the risk of getting burned. Kids being kids, Lynne was not paying attention and her flannel nightgown caught fire. She started running, which made the flames bigger and more uncontrollable. The fire got worse and Caesar immediately ran after Lynne, finally catching up to her. He worked like crazy putting out the fire, and doing so he got burned very badly on his hands and arms. Caesar's devotion to Lynne was so plain in that moment; he kept asking her if she was alright, not thinking about his own burned hands and arms. I thought nothing about this at the time, except this was what he was supposed to do.

Unfortunately, Caesar was not too keen on my brother Joe or me. He showed it by making life a living hell for both of us. He beat us something fierce for minor infractions such as failing to perform household chores, not moving fast enough when he called, rolling my eyes, talking under my breath, wetting the bed. Yes, I wet my bed until I was thirteen and a half years old. Joseph usually

13

bore the brunt of these beatings because he frequently tried to run away from home. When Caesar caught up to him, he would take Joseph out to the garage and severely punish him for his runaway attempts. I wasn't whipped as often as Joseph, but my whippings were just as severe. I reasoned that Caesar's violent punishment style was a result of the abuse he suffered as an effeminate male child. For him severe punishment was protocol; the way things were done. The cruel treatment Caesar inflicted upon Joe and me was the polar opposite of how he treated his own three sons Albert, Caesar Jr., and Keola. His disdain for me was certainly mutual. I stole change from his pockets all the time, because he never gave Joe and me anything. I thought Caesar was a joke. But, as I look back, I think maybe he was leaving that money there for us to get; like everyone else in Mother's realm, he was just as controlled as we were.

Caesar became a central part of the unfortunate "name game" that has plagued my children and me to this day. Christopher Bell was not my real father; Mother put his name on my birth certificate. This assignment of nominal paternity proved temporary. I went to school one Monday as Ollan Christopher Bell and by that Friday, *Arvanola* was married to Caesar and my surname was suddenly "James." As was usually the case with Arvanola's plans, the details were sketchy. Just as randomly as my surname was assigned it was changed in a blink of an eye. The intergenerational drama caused by this seemingly trivial name reassignment has not been as easy to correct, as it was to create. The fact that Mother ruled my life as a young man has caused me serious problems, which have not ended. I went into the U.S. Army using the surname James, yet, had the sergeant signing me up asked to see my birth certificate, I would have gone into the service as Ollan C. Bell, not Ollan C. James. This is the kind of power my mother had over people. It did not stop there; her will would take over and rule my very being.

2
Early Mornings In The Jordan Household

Prior to the arrival of my three younger half-brothers all the children in *Arvanola's* household typically awakened at five-thirty in the morning. Lynne, Joseph, Rosie, myself and any number of other children who would room with us over the years started our day with prayer, poetry, and music. Mother would play the piano and teach us songs. She instilled in us a love for music and show business early in our lives. Mother had a beautiful singing voice. She was my first voice teacher.

I studied the classic pop singers of the era, such as Dean Martin, Frank Sinatra, and Mel Torme, and received my musical education from my mother. Mother also made sure all of us children were well-versed in literature. She was particularly fond of reciting the classic, dark poetry of Edgar Allan Poe. Mother would not only read to us in the morning, but also before we went to bed. She would tell us stories about people coming from the grave; they were never violent or too scary.

Around this time I was introduced to my main instrument: the bass. My first makeshift bass consisted of an old silver-colored washtub, a handle of a broom, and a string. What Mother had me do was take a broom and cut a groove into the part that we had cut off, then put part of the stick on the edge of the wash tub, attach a string to it, and move it back and forth to get the sound I wanted.

Our household could have easily been mistaken for a boarding home. Mother took in so many families, mostly white single mothers and their children. Sometimes, my siblings and I grew annoyed with the inconvenience that came with the influx of strangers to our home. Mother would come home sometimes with other children to stay with us for a while. I am not sure how it worked back then but she would always bring them home in the middle of the night. We would have to get up and let them sleep in our beds. When I was real young, some kids came to the house and Mother told us to sleep in the back room. As always, I asked, "Why do we always have to get up?" She gave me a good ass whipping and made me get up. On one of those nights, after being rudely awakened, I learned how to tell time. Mother kept me up all night until I could tell time. This was when I started to like numbers, could remember numbers very quickly, and retain them for years. I can still remember significant numbers from my childhood.

Mother came home one day with a lady named Edna Harris. Ms. Harris had two children, a girl named Amanda and a boy named Freddie. Their features had me guessing; they were mixed American Indian and African American. I'm sure they were homeless, because they wouldn't have stayed with us as long as they did. One of the most striking things about them was their hair. They had the kind of hair my grandmother would call "good hair." Mother would rave about how beautiful their hair was. That didn't make me feel good about my own hair, which was coarse and markedly different from the Harris children's hair.

Each new family that came into our home brought new things; some were good and some not so good. Freddie was stealing food. He would do this even after he had eaten. He could have gone back for more, but he chose to do the negative thing. He didn't need to do that at all. He would take food and hide it under the mattress, then Mother would find it and all hell would break loose. Caesar was there during this time and beat him a lot for this at Mother's command. Freddie was also a bed-wetter, which was a problem for me because he slept with me. I would get pissed on all the time!

All kinds of things went on in the Jordan household. I remember the first time I smelled marijuana. My mother and grandmother were in the front room talking and smoking. I knew what cigarettes smelled like and, because marijuana grew wild in the backyard, I was familiar with that smell as well. They would roll it up in some paper and smoke it, and then the laughter would begin. But we were kids at that time and didn't know what was really going on. I did not smoke until I was out of the service, in 1966, several years later.

Many single mothers and their children who came through the house would stay with us for short periods of time. Others

16

stayed for months. Despite the constant comings and goings, I always felt that I was alone and there was something missing in my life. I never felt like a complete person. I always felt I was not good enough, and being called *Blackie* didn't help my self-esteem any. The only time I felt good as a child was when I was singing. I would clean the floors on my hands and knees, singing all the time while I was scrubbing.

3
Sex Games

As I experienced childhood in the 1940s and 50s, American society was on the verge of losing its collective innocence. The pent-up sexual frustrations of the Victorian era were soon to be agitated and ignited, teenage imaginations fueled by the likes of swaggering rock n' rollers such as Jackie Brenston, Big Joe Turner, Bullmoose Jackson, Chuck Berry, and Jackie Wilson. My discovery of sex was much more matter of fact. In 1949, the kids that frequented our house were clearly ahead of the game.

We were fascinated by the steady flow of new playmates, many of whom brought with them a level of sexual precocity previously foreign to us. Away from the watchful eye of grownups, we children acted upon our burgeoning sexual curiosity, playing with and exploring each other's bodies. As a result, sexual awareness came early on for me. When I was about six or seven, one little white girl pulled my zipper down and began to play with my private parts. I did not think about it. It was something that just happened, and I felt no anger, shame, or guilt. I felt it was a natural thing to do. We were never taught about sex from our parents, so we had no idea what was right or wrong when it came to appropriate sexual behavior. At around 12 years old we stopped this behavior.

One of the mothers that stayed with us for an extended period of time was Lillian, a single white woman with three daughters and a son: Ruth, Stella, Kathy, and Bobby. For some reason, Lillian took a liking to me when I was 13. She was always telling me how cute I was. Joseph and I were excited to have Ruth and Stella as new playmates for the sex games we had learned. Stella was all for the sex games; she would play with Joseph and me all the time, when no one was home, of course. Ruth would not think of participating. She did not like my mother very much. But they were around us for several years.

The negative effects of my formative years have plagued me as an adult. As I was learning the physical basics of sex at a very young age, there was no corresponding parental guidance to promote responsible sexual behavior. I was much older when they came to stay with us, so I knew what we were doing was not the right thing, but I enjoyed it. These types of things went on for several years and then I went to junior high school and started seeing other cute girls. Around this time both families had moved into their own homes, although Stella continued to come to the house to enjoy the games.

The games would become more intense and Joseph would always try to be the leader. Joseph was now a lot bigger than I was, so he would try to bully me into not playing the game, but Stella wanted to play with us both. She seemed to enjoy seeing us fight over her. In hindsight, our competition over Stella's affections was a harbinger of things to come, as adults. Although Stella was very pretty, I lost interest in her after a while. It wasn't worth the hassle with Joseph.

Neither one of us went all the way with Stella, but we would come close at times. I went on to high school, all the families went their own separate ways, and then I went into the Army. While I was in the Army, I learned that Stella passed away giving birth to a child. The father of the baby was a black man. When I got the news I was very sad because I liked Stella a lot and no matter what, she was a real sweet person. They tell me when a woman gives birth and passes away, at that time her soul goes to a good place. If that is true then Stella deserves this, as she was a good person.

4

Spirituality or "Black Art"

Spirituality in our household was no less fraught with confusion and ambiguity. In addition to the bedtime stories replete with graveyard resurrections, mother often held events at home, which were some type of hybrid between a prayer meeting and a séance. At these séances, mostly white attendees held hands as Mother used her powers to conjure the spirit of an individual's departed loved ones. My siblings and I watched, our young minds unsure of how to reconcile this otherworldly display with the messages we received in church that condemned this type of activity as devilry and "black art." As contradictory as the messages were, Christianity and reverence for the supernatural peacefully coexisted in our household. My grandmother reinforced the superstitions. For instance, every morning Mama made a point to take a slop jar, a jar used as a makeshift urinal at night when one did not feel like walking to the bathroom, and pour the evening's collection on the front porch prior to anyone leaving the house to ward off evil spirits. As a child I had terrible nightmares and wet the bed a lot, fearful that some ghost would get me before the night was over.

We kids spent a lot of time in church. We were members of a Holiness church, and bound by its strict teachings. We used to go to church on Saturday to "march for Jesus," as my mother put it. We spent most of the Sabbath at church, marching for the Lord. We read the Bible and studied verses over and over, until we could say them by heart. Mother also took correspondence courses and became a minister. Armed with her new qualification, she held classes and prayer meetings at home. Attendance was mandatory for *Arvanola's* children.

The religious aspect of my upbringing, though confusing, contributed to a strong sense of discipline that remains with me to this day. I remember Mother was giving a reading to some woman when we were staying at my grandfather's house on Center Street. Houses back then were built with round fronts, so there were round shapes between the windowpanes. There was a very nice-sized space between the window and the curtains. My sister Lynne and I sat behind this curtain and were told not to make a sound, while my mother was giving the reading. At the end of the reading Mother pulled back the curtain and said, with satisfaction, "This is what I call discipline." The lady my mother was giving the reading to was shocked because we never made a sound, for God knows how long. To pass the time and make silence more bearable, Lynne and I would roll an eraser back and forth, eager for the reading to be over so we could play under less restrictive conditions.

The contradictory messages of religion and the spirit world were confusing, leaving me with yet another set of questions to be answered later in life. We spent a lot of time, in some way or another, in church, for whatever it was worth. But with the same breath we would deal with the supernatural side of things. This is the part I could never understand. I figured that it was one way or the other, God or the spirit world, but don't give me both. I could not handle it.

I observed many contradictions and double standards in my young life, courtesy of Grandmother and Mother. Being the mouthy little boy that I was, I often called my elders on their contradictions. There was a double standard when it came to being truthful. We were taught to never tell a lie but this only applied when we were talking to my mother, my grandmother, and my aunts. It was not a problem when it came to lying to outsiders such as neighbors, schoolmates, teachers, etc. Frequently, Mother and Grandmother urged us kids to tell little white lies to outsiders, to save their own skin. As a literal young man, I could not reconcile their orders to lie with the general rule that prohibited lying. Once, all of us kids were playing outside the A Street house, and my grandmother had a friend down the street named Mrs. Wheeler. Mama said "If Mrs. Wheeler comes by tell her I'm not here." I replied, "Well, you said we should always tell the truth." Mama laughed and shrugged it off, saying, "You heard me, boy!" So, when Mrs. Wheeler came by and asked "Is your grandmother home?" I replied, "Yes, she is. Just knock on the door." The whole time I was saying "Yes" my sister Lynne was saying "No." As you may have guessed, I got my ass beat again.

"Lord, What Did I Do For You To Make Me So Black and Blue?"
– Fats Waller

My level of interaction with white people during my childhood was considerably high for a young Black boy in that era. There were always new people in our life and in our house, and most of them were white. The first girl I ever kissed was a white girl: her name was Elaine Smith. Except for my family, most of the people I relate to tend to be white. Some of the harsh racial realities experienced by Black Americans on the industrial East Coast and in the rural south were completely foreign to this kid from Oakland. This is ironic, in light of some of the socially conscious tunes I sang with the Natural Four, such as our remake of the Temptations' "Message from A Black Man," James Brown's anthem "I'm Black and I'm Proud" and "Stepping On Up."

As a member of the Natural Four I was presented to the world as a young man full of racial pride. My "natural" stands perfectly groomed upon my head, a living, breathing testament to the hip phrases of that day: "Black is Beautiful," "Happy to be Nappy" and "Dig Yourself." The 1960s and 70s soul era that gave rise to groups like the Natural Four, was a powerful ode to Black men. Popular groups like The Temptations and solo acts like Jackie Wilson offered a new brand of idols. These tall, handsome, and talented stars, some dangerously sexy and others clean-cut church boys, made Black men of all complexions sex symbols to women of all races. Unfortunately, the new appreciation of darker complexions was still a distant fantasy during my childhood. I was frequently taunted in my youth for being dark-skinned, enduring such indignities as being called "Blackie" and "Ugly." Unlike the image I presented, inside I was self-conscious about my blackness from my hair to my darker hue.

Within my own family, my dark complexion was a liability about which I received a constant reminder. My sister, *Rosie* received preferential treatment from my grandmother because of her lighter skin. Rose was Mama's pet, so she spent most of her time at home with her. She was always either sick or playing sick. When I commented about Rose's favored status, Mama would give me a whipping or put me on my knees on rice in a corner. Rosie never studied; she would say, 'I don't feel well" and then would be home for a week or two. The tension between Rosie and I persists to this day. We hardly even talk, and we never spend time together. I see her very seldom.

Grandmother (*Mama*), a fair-skinned Indian/Black woman, frequently spoke ill of dark, Black people, even though she married a dark-skinned man. The advice I received from Grandmother reinforced what I believed to be the inherent undesirability of dark skin. She warned me to never marry a dark-skinned person, since I was dark myself lest the children come out "black and ugly." "Never marry a black woman because your kids will grow up to have nappy hair," she said. This was a complex that Mama had about hair; I was already jacked up because I realized that I had the kind of hair she so despised. My hair was coarse and hard to comb, so most of the time she or my mother would use a hot comb to make it straight, burning my scalp in the process.

We were taught that if you had nappy hair you should do everything you could to straighten it. There were times my mother would send me to school with my hair straightened and it would rain and my hair would revert back. The other kids would laugh at me in school. Not only was I dark, but also I had the kind of hair that my Grandmother and Mother said you shouldn't have. One thing I carried into my adulthood was giving myself a perm. My friend Bobby Keys, and I would try giving each other perms; sometimes it was painful. Someone told me that you could use lye and potato mixed together, and that this would work. I found out the hard way that those of us using these two ingredients were misinformed on the highest level. It burned our heads so bad we would have sores on our heads for weeks. I learned to use the right products available in the stores. I started buying this product called King Conk, a hair relaxer preferred by popular artists of the era like Jackie Wilson, Wilson Pickett, John Lee Hooker, and Sam Cooke. In the early days, so did the Natural Four.

My mother had a full head of hair that was not so curly, as it was more like my grandmother's. My brother Joseph and sister Rose had full heads of hair. I was the only one cursed with this "bad hair." Today, I have no hair at all. I think it's because of all I had done to my hair in my younger days. I also found out much later in life that hair does not make a person. I wish I had learned that lesson years ago. I would have hair today!

5
Punishment

Adding insult to injury, I often voluntarily took the fall for my siblings. I offered to take the whippings intended for Joseph or *Rosie* simply because I was not in the mood to hear the constant screaming between Mother and Grandmother. Mother would line us up to give us whippings. And if you moved she had this cane and she'd pull you back with it. I figured that offering to take the whippings for all of my sisters and brothers would end it, but it didn't work out that way. Mother would give me all their whippings, and then turn around and whip them anyway. Even after I assumed the older brother's responsibility for correcting my younger siblings when they misbehaved, I was often punished. One day, all of us kids were playing and my sister *Rosie*, as always, was being the ass that my grandmother made her into, so I got on her case. My grandmother did not like the way I spoke to my sister so she wet her hand in cold water and slapped me so hard that my ear rang for days afterwards.

Along with the negative messages force-fed to me concerning my hair and complexion, these childhood incidents had the cumulative effect of making me feel trapped in my own skin at times. Between my dark skin and the way I was treated because of it, I began to feel that my situation would be better if only I was lighter. To this day, I feel deep within myself I was born the wrong color. It has taken me years to understand and come to terms with the fact that colorism existed within my own family. I feel I lost a lot because of my color. I feel if I had been another color or another race, things would have gone better for me. I have mixed feelings about being an African American. I've had these feelings some years now. It is one of those things that will be with me until the day I die. It becomes depressing at times and I try to think of other things.

6
Bullies

Childhood was rough for me in school, too. I was a very small boy, making me a perfect target for neighborhood bullies. After a quarrel between Grandmother and *Arvanola*, we all went to 819 Center Street to live with Papa. Mother enrolled me in Cole Elementary School. On my first day at Cole Mother put a blue hat on my head and told me not to lose it. So I went into the classroom with the hat on and the teacher told me to take it off. I told him my mother said not to lose the hat, so I cannot take it off. Back then, if your teacher said for you to do something and you did not do as they said they could take a ruler and hit you on your hand, or across your backside. The teacher snatched the hat from my head and smacked my hand with a ruler. This was the first time I had been hit in school by someone other than my grandmother, so right after he hit me I got up and ran home. I told Mother what happened and, naturally, in response, she took me back to school and confronted the teacher. I went back to school the next day and the teacher was not very pleased with the fact that my mother had confronted him, and the rest of the class was laughing. So, he made everyone stay after class because of me, who he referred to as "Mr. Bell." The teacher began allowing students to leave in small groups, at the end of the day. The bullies left first, eager to get their hands on the runt with the big mouth.

I knew it was not going to be a good day. I was a fast runner, very little and very scared. Sensing that I was about to meet my impending doom, I begged the teacher to let me stay in the classroom a little longer to avoid the bullies. The teacher laughed at my request and sent me on my way. We lived about six blocks away from Cole School so I had no choice but to think of a way to get home without getting my ass beat. The second they turned their heads I took off running. The teacher knew what was happening but just looked out the window as I ran by. Thankfully, I was a very quick runner. I saw a hole in the fence, so I jumped through it. The bullies had to go around, so that gave me enough time to get some distance between us. I hit the corner and headed up Center Street with them coming up fast. I ran into the house, screaming for my grandfather. He ran to get his shotgun and went to the door. The next day I was back at 8801 A Street, in Highland School.

Although the environment at Highland was an improvement from Cole, it didn't offer a total escape from the bullies. Some of the bullies would turn me upside down and shake my little money out of my pocket, then put me in the garbage can and sit on it until the yard teacher stopped them. One of the other kids would tell the yard teacher; otherwise, I would be in the can for a while. This one kid, Leroy Hackett, would do this to me all the time. He was very big; even the yard teacher was afraid of him. Aside from coming up with inventive ways to avoid bullies, grammar school was an uneventful time for me. Though I was always a smart and well-spoken young man, I concede I was a terrible student. I was adept at math and learned some things that would serve me well in the future, but academics were not a top priority. My grammar school days were spent just trying to get through classes and learn stories about white people and the history of America.

Another skill I learned indirectly from school was the ability to tolerate bullies. I would encounter them all of my life. The bullying didn't stop in my youthful days, but continued on into my adult life, and even as a member of The Natural Four. There were times when *Punkin*, the leader of the group when I joined, and I would get into it over how his selling drugs could jeopardize the group. Because this was not my lifestyle I felt that his dealings would lead to us going to jail, or getting killed, for some crazy reason.

Punkin was a bully, six feet and one inch tall, around 200 pounds, and loved to fight. When I joined the group I didn't know this. We never got into a fight but there were times when we came close to having it out. Then came Delmos, and the same thing continued. It seemed like I brought these kinds of actions out of people, not that I wanted to fight. It was just the way I talked. I guess the biggest bully of them all was my mother. She totally bullied me all my life. Even in death, she bullied me from the grave. Even today I wonder if I will ever be free from her bullying spirit. I think not, and that is why I consider her the most hurtful person in my life. I ask myself "how can a mother do the things she did to her

27

son and then turn right around and say, 'I love you?'" She took away my freedom, held me emotionally hostage, abused me physically, and yet said she loved me. I guess I will never know the answer, and it makes me sick inside.

7
Pleasant Memories

Elementary school was boring for me. Mother didn't help a lot with homework because she worked long hours. My grandmother never helped so we had to do a lot on our own. Junior high school was similarly a blur for me. I began singing in the choir and I learned how to type. I took up cooking instead of shop so I was called a sissy, but this didn't bother me because cooking class was where all the girls were.

My childhood was not without pleasant moments. My grandfather picked me up one day and took me to the merry-go-round in San Francisco. I was very little so the memory is vague, at best, but this was the best time of my life. There are times when I remember my grandmother fondly, as well, particularly her cooking, a talent that she passed along to me. I also discovered my affinity for music and my vocal talent, during my childhood. One of my happiest memories was winning a red ribbon in a talent contest for performing the song "At the Cross" when 12 years old. It is an old gospel song with these words,
At the Cross at the Cross, where I first saw the light and the burdens of my heart flew away, It was there by faith I received my sight, and now I am happy all the day.
This is the first verse, and the only one I remember well. The win was a great thrill for me, and a taste of things to come.

The discovery of music, as a child, undoubtedly, was the most important one of my life. Not only would my talent provide me with a fulfilling lifelong career but I also found an unerring friend. When everything dramatic was happening in my life I would get deeper into my music. Amidst the family drama and fatiguing struggle to make it, the music was always there to console me. In high school my affinity for music flourished. I enjoyed the choir and under the tutelage of my instructor, James Snyder, my vocal ability blossomed. I performed songs from classic musicals like *South Pacific* and *Porgy and Bess.* Singing with the choir was a wonderful oasis for me, and it allowed me to strengthen my bond with music. At home, my musical training was supplemented by pop radio. I listened to and learned from those smooth pop crooners like Dean Martin, Frank Sinatra and Mel Torme. I also loved listening to country music. Eventually, as a teenager, with my discovery of Sam Cooke's soulful vocal stylings, I discovered rhythm and blues. Ricky Nelson ranks as one of my all-time most influential singers. Brook Benton and Johnny Mathis were also personal favorites, and Johnny Cash was a favorite of my grandmother's and mine, too. I learned to like his style, along with Willie Nelson. We listened to a lot of country and western music in my house. The music in the house though was not just pop, gospel, country and soul. We also listened to classical music. This was all part of the learning process.

8
From Track To R.O.T.C.

I put the speed I developed from avoiding bullies to good use by running track in high school. I was not too popular, not the fastest runner on the track team, and there were the same bullies fucking with me. We had a track meet and I was told to run the relays and be the anchor. I was also told by all of the other runners not to fuck up or else I'd get my ass kicked. This made me feel real good about doing this. I had never run a relay before, and did not know how to accept the baton. During the race, I slowed down so I could get the baton; it hit the ground and the other teams took off and left me. I tried to catch up but this was not going to happen. I ran around the track and there was an open fence. I dropped the baton and ran into the armory and joined the R.O.T.C. that same day.

The R.O.T.C. (Reserve Officer's Training Corps) is where I started my first singing group, along with two other R.O.T.C. students, Bobby Keys and Robert Jackson. We named ourselves The Underwood's, inspired by the brand of typewriters we used in our typing class. Our three-man group never recorded anything, but we would harmonize to popular songs on the radio as well as gospel songs in between R.O.T.C. exercises. Our first real gigs were at Castlemont High, the school we attended at the time, and Greater Emanuel Church of God In Christ in Oakland, where I was forced to go on Saturdays to march for Jesus. We were together maybe six months before all of us went our own separate ways. Bobby joined the Army. Robert became a minister of a large church in Oakland, called Acts Full Gospel, and I went into the service and continued to sing. I'm the only one of us who stayed in this crazy business of music. I sang in a few other churches, such as Parks Chapel, particularly in Oakland. I always found myself doing some music.

9
Dating: Dollar a Kiss

My early days as a young adult interacting with the opposite sex were hit or miss, but mostly miss. My first unofficial girlfriend was a young lady from my church, named Marjorie. I would give her the money that I was supposed to put in the collection plate so she would talk to me. She said that she would be my girlfriend if I didn't tell anyone and of course, I agreed. When I visited her house, other guys would be there. I would just wait until she finished doing whatever she was doing with them and then I'd take her to my house on my bike. We would read the Bible with my mother. I did not realize how dumb I was at the time, and not the best boyfriend to have.

High school dating was the source of my most humiliating teenage moments. The night my mother took me to my senior prom, she gave me a dollar and ten cents. The dollar was to buy a Coke for my date and me and the dime was to call home when the prom was over so she could pick me up. It was humiliating to have all of my brothers and sisters in the car as Mother drove up to the auditorium. I felt like a clown.

I fared no better with a young lady named Ivory, another in my never-ending saga with dating as a very young man, and my most memorable high school girlfriend. She was a beautiful, very dark-skinned young lady. I took Ivory to the Military Ball and she was dressed up so beautiful. I had on my newly pressed R.O.T.C. dress uniform and thought I was looking good. All the guys wanted to dance with her and I said "okay," being the gentleman that I was. About halfway through the dance, I saw a short line of guys and there was Ivory, selling kisses for a dollar. The guys were buying them as fast as she would kiss them. When it came time to take Ivory home, I asked for a kiss and she refused. I asked why I couldn't have a kiss, and she said, "You can, for a dollar." These were the kinds of things that happened to me most of my young life.

Things have changed a lot as an adult, although some things never change. I always seemed to be spending money on women just to keep them in my life. How sad was that? I tried to change that, but, for some reason, I still believed I had to buy my way into love. When I met a woman who showed me some attention I would pay to go to bed with her. I would buy her gifts, take her on trips and buy her affection.

10
Welcome to the Real World

After graduating from high school in 1961, I attended Laney Junior College for about six months. I was in a band for a while, singing and playing percussion. I soon became disenchanted with my studies. I had always been somewhat ambivalent as far as academics were concerned. Bringing in money and keeping busy were foremost on my mind. I took a job working for one of my mother's friends, which was a big mistake. I had not caught on to the fact that mother was still in charge of my life. Jim Cowdrey, one of mother's clients at the time, owned a brick masonry company and put me on his payroll for about three months as a general laborer. Mother always pocketed most of my earnings, as she had since I was a boy delivering newspapers and cutting grass. I was never allowed to keep even half the money I made. However, I was now an 18 year old young man, ready to lead my own life, with my own money. At least I thought I was. Three months into the job with Mr. Cowdrey, I decided it was time to leave home and finally escape my mother's ironclad rule. That was when I decided to join the Army.

I informed mother of my intention to enlist. She promptly took me down to the recruiting office and I received the standard information on the benefits of joining the military. I took the S.A.T. (Scholastic Aptitude Test) for the entrance exam and failed. A week later Mother went down to the recruiter's office, and then she told me to go back down there, and I did. I don't know what was said, but they signed me up and I was in the Army. Strangely, Army recruiters allowed me to enlist under the last name of James when, in fact, my birth certificate showed me as "Ollan Christopher Bell."

I never understood what Mother said to get them to bypass the name on my birth certificate and enlist me as James. The one thing I was sure of was that Mother had a lot to do with it. Even though I signed up as a recruit, and was supposed to be a man, my mother still pulled all the strings. She had arranged for me to give her 50% of the money I made in the Army, which was not very much to begin with. It became clear that joining the Army did not change anything. The power she had over me would not allow me to regain control of my life, to be free from her firm grip for a very long time.

BERKELEY HOSPITAL
A non-profit association
2001 DWIGHT WAY
BERKELEY, CALIFORNIA

HOSPITAL BIRTH CERTIFICATE

This Certifies that

OLLAN CHRISTOPHER BELL

Was born in this Hospital at 12:05 *o'clock* A. M. June 15, 1943

No. P43-274

Family History

Father's Name Christopher Bell
Residence 819 Center Street, Oakland
Birthplace Pennsylvania Date 1914
Mother's Maiden Name Earlyne Odelle Jordan
Birthplace California Date 1920
Place of marriage of parents Pittsburg, California
Sex of Child Male weight at birth 7 lbs. 9 ozs.

In Witness Whereof the said Hospital has caused this Certificate to be signed by its duly authorized officer and by the attending physician and has hereunto affixed its seal.

F.T. Read, M. Attending Physician

Alfred E. Mai Superintendent

Baby's Footprint · Mother's Right Thumbprint

Once enlisted, I was sent to Fort Ord, California. Fort Ord was located on Highway 1, about five miles north of Monterey. I did my first eight weeks of basic training there. I excelled as a GI in training. Between all the marching for Jesus, the R.O.T.C., and Mother giving out orders, I had received my first military training long before, at home and in high school. After successful completion of the Army's basic training, I graduated and discovered I would soon be leaving the confines of Oakland for the very first time. Mother and my siblings all attended my graduation, and I was gleeful at the thought of finally leaving home and experiencing the world on my own for the first time. I took one more trip home about two weeks later and said my goodbyes. I was headed to Fort Chaffee, Arkansas, located in the city of Fort Smith.

Arvenola's grduation

Ollan & Mother

Ollan

Mother, Lynne, Ollan, Joe
CJ, Rose & Albert

C.J.

Albert

Ollan & Lynne

Lynne

Albert, Ollan & Joe

Lynne & Ollan

Foster Kids w/
Ollan, Lynne & Joe

Stella

Lynne & Ollan

Keola

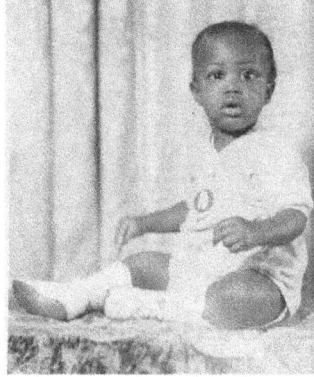
Ollan

Ollan on bike

Rose

Ollan

Bobby keys
My best friend

Ollan & Joe

Lynne & Ollan

Ollan, Lynne & Joe

Ollan & Joe

Ollan & Joe

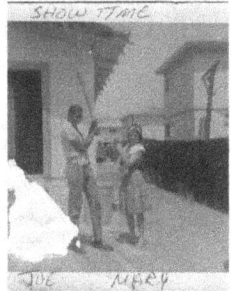

Joe & Mary

Joe
Lynne
Ollan

Lynn, Joe & Ollan

Ollan

11
Down South

I will never forget this trip. It was mostly good, but it was the first time I ever encountered overt racism. We were on a troop train headed to Fort Smith, Arkansas, and had to pass through the town of Texarkana, Texas. The train stopped and the troops were told to get off so we could eat. We got off the train, about 200 GI's total. They had us line up and we headed to this restaurant. We went inside and started to sit down when one of the waitresses informed us we couldn't eat there. The officer in charge said something and we ended up leaving the restaurant and headed to a place across the street where they pulled the drapes so no one could see us. We ate and got ready to leave. Walking out, we saw that down the street a group of about 50 or 60 white men with sticks and chains were headed for us. To avoid an altercation, the officer instructed the troops to quickly board the train. We pulled out of Texarkana, leaving me to think about my first brush with racism the rest of the way to Arkansas.

Once at Fort Chaffee, I discovered what my job in the military would entail. I was listed as a clerk typist and medical records clerk because I had experience with typing from high school. As I prepared for my six-month tour of duty, things were good; I was not at home, and my mother was not running my life. I did not have to worry about my brothers and sisters. I did not have to see Caesar. Life was good and I was free. I was there about two months, and made some new friends. We used to hang out in the day room or the P.X. (Post Exchange). We sang, I played piano, we drank beer and shot pool.

12
Jail

One night I went to a party in the town of Fort Smith with a couple of other GIs, one in particular named Strickland. He was a big guy. We went to this house party in the Black part of town, and were there about two hours. Things were good at first, and then a little later Strickland said we had to leave. We were in my car, a 1950 Ford I bought from some sergeant on the Post. I asked Strickland why we had to leave. He said "I will tell you later, just get going." We headed out of the party. Everyone was running so I ran also. We jumped in the car and I went to the driver's side. Ron, one of the other guys, asked if I could let him drive. He took the keys and started to drive fast. I asked him again what was going on and that's when I saw the gun. I went straight to panic city as we were driving fast and the cops were coming up behind us.

We continued speeding down the road with the cops in hot pursuit. Ron handed the gun to Strickland and he was getting ready to throw it out of the window. I thought he was trying to shoot at the cops so I tried to stop him. He yelled that he was trying to throw the gun away. This was 1962, in the deep part of the South. Even as naïve as I was, I knew this was not the right place for a Black man to have a gun while running from the police. The cops finally pulled us over and we went to jail. The only thing that saved us was the fact we were GIs. We landed in hot water when we returned to the base, and ended up doing extra duty, receiving an Article 15, a form of non-judicial punishment that consisted of our pay being docked. The incident also went on our records.

When my stint at Fort Chaffee came to an end, I was shipped out to Fort Polk, Louisiana, where I served as a general morning clerk and a medical clerk. I handled paperwork in the morning and processed the soldiers coming in and out of the company. At almost 19 years old, I was suddenly miles away from the racially integrated, easy-going environment of Oakland, California. My naiveté was evident. Even though experiences in Texarkana and Fort Chaffee showed me that my integrated upbringing was not the norm in these parts it would take a few more false starts before I adjusted to this new, decidedly raw way of life. I went to a bar one night with a white military friend of mine and was promptly told to leave. I walked away from the experience bewildered, wondering what type of place wouldn't permit someone to drink at a bar. It was the first time in my life that I was actually barred from hanging out with white people.

Music remained high on my agenda during my time at Fort Polk. I played a little piano and sang during my leisure time with my musically-inclined friends. The guys I hung out with at the post were also singers, and together we performed on the weekends. Our exciting performances garnered the interest of the ladies, an added benefit of my musical talent. This was the best part of being in the service, for me. This was the time I also thought I had grown up and should have been a man, but I would find out, as time went on, that this was not the case. Mother was still in charge, and I would have to deal with that, always.

13
A Lady of the Night

At Fort Polk I had my first encounter with a prostitute. I was in the very small town of Leesville. There were no sidewalks, just a dirt road that led to the railroad tracks where we would catch the bus to go back to the post. This was yet another culture shock for this naïve boy from the big city of Oakland. There were several places we could hang out, but the best place for young men like me was a place called Annie May's. It was a very small bar, a juke joint that served Coca Cola and other soft drinks, and had a jukebox that played the latest songs from most of the Black artists like Fats Domino, Ray Charles, Rufus Thomas, Etta James, The Shirelles, the Four Tops, the Miracles, Stevie Wonder, Martha Reeves and the Vandellas, just to name a few. Across the street from Annie May's there was a metal building shaped like a barn. This was the place where prostitutes set up shop to service the GIs during their off-duty hours. At the time a self-described "square," I decided to venture across the street to see what this place was all about. A large, physically imposing man was there to greet me at the door, asking impatiently, "What do you want?" I let the man know I was just looking, to which he responded, "Do you want to buy something, or not?"

Just browsing, apparently, was not an option at this joint. The choices the man laid out for me were to either "Buy or get the fuck out of here." After exchanging a few more words with the giant doorman I decided upon the latter and headed back across the street to Annie May's. I happened to glance over my shoulder and noticed a very cute young lady from the metal barn-shaped building across the street coming my way, hot on my heels, asking if I wanted to buy some. Politely, I turned down the generous offer of sexual service. This cute young lady chased me, encouraged by her pimp yelling for her to "Get that motherfucker." Just before I could reach the safety of Annie May's the young lady caught up with me and grabbed my jacket. She only managed to grab my belt on the back of it, ripping it off. My coat was ruined but my virginity remained intact, for the time being. She kept repeating "Only ten and two baby, only ten and two!" which was business shorthand for ten dollars for the lady and two for the room.

I finally made it into Annie May's and, thankfully, lost my would-be sex-benefactor, who did not attempt to follow me inside. This was a safe place for GIs like me, new to the world. We were content to enjoy a Coke and dance with the young ladies who were church-going kind of girls. It was a place we could listen to songs of Jackie Wilson, Sam Cooke, Brook Benton and many others. This was a wonderful thing. I spent a lot of time at Annie May's.

14

My First True Relationship (Loreatha)

It was at Annie May's, that haven for "good girls and square guys," where I met my first real girlfriend, Loreatha Thomas. Loreatha was a plain-looking, brown-skinned country girl, with full, lips and a cute, keen nose. I recall with great pleasure her inviting smile and bright eyes. She was a very nice girl. She had skinny little legs, which I'll never forget. We got along very well; it was my first real relationship. In addition to her cute shape and pleasant looks, little Loreatha knew her way around the kitchen. In fact, the first meal she ever made for me was an introduction to country cuisine: possum, black-eyed peas, and cornbread. Though Loreatha kept me well-fed, at this point I was more interested in making it with a girl. Unfortunately for my libido, sweet Loreatha was adamant about her rule against sex until marriage, which was quite ironic considering her mother was a prostitute.

Loreatha and I dated for about six months. Throughout our relationship my friends at the base constantly bombarded me with questions concerning whether I had yet scored with her. While things with my Loreatha were moving along smoothly, I yearned to go beyond the standard heavy-petting repertoire of kissing, hugging, and touching. I bought an engagement ring, intending to propose to her. I informed Mother and Grandmother of my intent to marry and sent a picture of my prospective fiancée back home. Mother gave her blessing, noncommittedly, saying it was okay if that's what I wanted.

Although I was content with my new plan to marry Loreatha, and the opportunity to *finally* seal the deal with her, my friends were not entirely happy with the idea of my continued holdout. One day, they got so sick of hearing the answer "No" to their questions of whether I had yet made it with Loreatha that they took it upon themselves to get me laid and have me lose my virginity, once and for all.

Loreatha Thomas

15
The Guidry Girls

We took a road trip about 60 miles away from the post to Lake Charles, Louisiana. Once within city limits we drove up Lincoln Street, a little road with no sidewalks and an acrid smell. We stopped in front of a dilapidated shack belonging to the Guidrys, a large Creole family. Two or three of the Guidry sisters stood outside, as though they were expecting us. My friends and I ventured inside the little shack, where I discovered ten or more children roaming about. It was a surprise to find so many children crammed into that two-bedroom house. It lacked hot running water and there was no bathroom inside. During that first meeting with the Guidry family, their father was in a drunken sleep on the couch and there was a big brown horse in the back of the house.

My friends Stewart, Pipcon, and McGinnis knew the Guidry sisters already. The Guidry girls would often entertain GIs to put food on the table. I was basically along for the good time. One of the Guidry sisters, Mary, was not so sociable on that first meeting. She lingered in the corner, radiating a real bad attitude. The guys and girls decided to keep the fun going and they set out for a night on the town. Mary, the sister with the funky attitude, sat out this trip and I thought nothing more of it. Before we left out we met Laura, the woman from next door who kept things moving along smoothly. She allowed the use of her home for personal business in exchange for a nominal fee.

Shortly after the road trip to Lake Charles and that initial meeting with the Guidry family, I headed back to Leesville to see Loreatha. Things went along well for a while between us, and I was still enjoying her good Southern cooking. Unfortunately for Loreatha, three weeks later Mary visited the post with her sisters. My friends and I accompanied the Guidry girls to the Post Exchange, its formal name, where there was a place to drink, dance, and generally have a good time. Mary seemed to have shed the surliness she displayed when I first met her. The night Mary and her sisters came down to the post, she was all-of-a-sudden on me like a cheap suit. As she was being extra nice and friendly toward me, I began to like this forward, Creole, light-skinned girl.

The Guidry girls headed back to Lake Charles after the evening's festivities were over, and I headed back to my main squeeze, more ready for sex than ever. I persisted in asking Loreatha for sex, and she remained unwavering in her commitment to saying "No." Suddenly, Mary was looking like more of an option for me. She kept dropping not-so-subtle hints that if I wanted sex she was more than willing to end my curiosity on the subject. My innocent relationship with Loreatha was coming to an end and I was about to enter into my first truly adult relationship. The mystery would be solved, once and for all; I was about to score.

As my curiosity grew stronger and Mary's hints turned into blatant come-ons, the visits to Loreatha became scarce. Sex with Mary was eminent, and Loreatha's sparkling personality was not enough for me to ignore the prospect. I did not officially break up with Loreatha, but rather, stopped coming around. Loreatha most likely did not know what to make of my gradual disappearance from her life. I never saw Loreatha after that, but I do think about the time I spent with her, and it makes me smile at how innocent it all was. I wish I had the chance to tell her that. Many years after I ended the relationship with Loreatha, I ran into a friend of hers in California, and asked how Loreatha had been making out. Her friend informed me that my disappearing act broke her heart. In hindsight, I don't think we would have lasted past my time in Fort Polk. She wanted to stay in Louisiana, and I knew I wasn't coming back once I left.

16
Mary

As the relationship with my first love was coming to an end I got things going with Mary. After sleeping with Mary for the first time I realized I enjoyed sex very much. But soon I started seeing her true colors, and then she never liked me. Our relationship, which began largely out of my sexual curiosity and Mary's corresponding willingness, was doomed from the start.

Shortly after becoming intimate with Mary I contracted a sexually transmitted disease. (STD) The morning of that awful discovery was one of intense emotions. I thought for sure God was punishing me for having sex and leaving Loreatha the way I did. I went back to the post and a few days later I began having problems urinating. I asked one of the guys what was happening to me and he said "Man, you got the clap." That was the term used back in the day for gonorrhea. Since I worked in medical records, I immediately knew what that meant. I went back to Lake Charles and confronted Mary. Mary acted like she didn't know what I was talking about, but her sisters Evelyn and Barbara knew and took me to a doctor they used when this type of situation arose. Normally, this would have been a clear sign to anyone that this person was not right. However, being the dummy I was, I kept on seeing Mary. I still had this feeling that it was my fault I had contracted the STD, and Mary stuck to her story that she was clean, even though her sisters told me she did go to get a shot.

I continued to see Mary. I sent a picture of us to my mother, which was the biggest mistake I could have made. Mother and my grandmother were overjoyed because Mary was "the right color." She had the right kind of hair and a very fair-skinned complexion, almost white.

Several months later I was shipped out to Germany, but first I returned home to say my good-byes to my family. Mother was exceptionally happy, and so was Mama, because I had landed a damn-near white girl. While I was at home I told Mother that I did not want to marry Mary, because I was not ready for marriage and I needed time to see what was going to happen in my life. Mother said that this young lady seemed very nice, was quite pretty, and that I should consider staying with her. I told my mother I had not had a chance to see other parts of the world, and that maybe I would think about it. I wanted the opportunity to see other people before I committed to this person.

The thing that was always looming in my mind was how I should tell Mother that Mary had given me a STD; maybe this would have changed her mind about Mary. But, knowing how she thinks, she would have probably told me to stay with her since we had been having sex. I was not thinking about what Mother wanted. I needed time to adjust to single life and expressed this over and over again, but it fell on deaf ears. All my mother could think about was the color of Mary's skin and the texture of her hair. So I just let things go for the next couple of days, thinking, "I will do what I want with whom I want when the time comes, because soon I will be in another country and in control of my own life." This was not to happen.

17
Shipping Out

After serving a little over six months at Fort Polk I was about to be transferred to another base, with the looming possibility of being sent to Vietnam. I headed home to Oakland and spoke with my mother about Mary, telling her that I had reservations about marriage. I was not ready to have a wife. I reiterated that my life was just beginning and I was not ready for a family. Mother reassured me that she understood and not to worry. When I left home this time I was sure I was in charge of my life. I felt I had spoken to mother as an adult, letting her know I was not ready for a commitment like this right now. I would find out later that my mother had plans already set and I was going to marry this fair-skinned girl from Louisiana, no matter what I had said to her. I was then sent to Fort Knox, Kentucky for about two weeks while I was in transit. After that, I left for Fort Dix, New Jersey, where I learned I would be sent to Germany. I boarded a military vessel called *The Patch*, the first boat I had ever been on, and it was very exciting. At that time I did not know that Mother was already in touch with Mary and the plan was already in motion. Oblivious to it all, I started a band with some of the other musically-inclined GIs, and we performed during the entire two-week trip to Germany.

When I got to Germany I was stationed at Kelly Barracks, which housed an airborne unit. Everyone had to go to jump school, but my band traveled around Germany playing for the troops instead. My first six months in Germany were most life-changing for me. I saw a world of nothing but white people. This was not strange to me; it was as it should be, in my mind. It felt like I had come home. Seeing all of those beautiful girls, I knew I was in the right place at the right time. I settled into the barracks, checked out the base, met my roomies and went to my job, all the things you do when you first get a job or a new place to live. As a medic, I could pretty much come and go as I pleased. The loose schedule of my job assignment gave me the opportunity to thoroughly check out the local music scene.

You're In The Army Now

Preparing for show in Germany

My first bass

Playing bass "The Capris"

"Soul Brother Band"

Soul Brother Band

The guitar I made into a bass

Fort Chaffey Ark - 1962

1962

Ready for my date with Helga

Heading to work

Heading to PX with friend

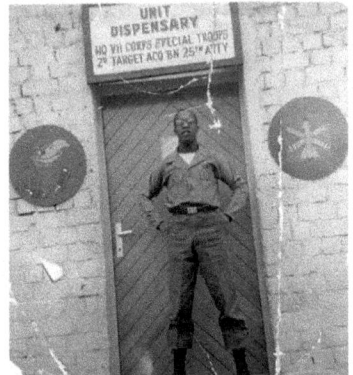

My first pair of Glasses

Ollan C. Bell PFC

At the club with Todd

Helga & Me

On the beach with Hiawatha

18
Helga

After a month or so in Germany I was at a venue called the Fifty Meter Club. At this club there was a house band playing two or three nights a week. There was a drummer named Charles McGuiness, a bass player named Sergeant Johnson, a guitar player named Marvin, from Oakland, California, and a singer named Jeff. Jeff was the regular singer so I would just sit in every so often, and the band knew that I played a little bass. I seized the opportunity to hone my singing style, singing and playing with the band from time to time.

At the Fifty Meter Club I met Helga, and had my first encounter with a German woman. We started dating and I could not believe how wonderful it was to be in a place where the girls liked me this much. She drove a black Pontiac Thunderbird convertible, picking me up on the weekends with the top down. Everyone on post would trip because she was so good-looking. My white military colleagues were not too pleased with Helga choosing me as her man. I quickly became the subject of their dirty looks, but it didn't matter. I enjoyed Helga very much; she spoke very good English and was a great lover. We went out to eat and to places that I would never have gotten to see otherwise. One of the most unique things about her was she liked to make love under the streetlights. Between the romantic rides through the country and hot evenings under the streetlights of Stuttgart, I had come a long way from being refused kisses at the doorstep. It was a wonderful time in my life. I was a young Black man from Oakland, California, in a different country, on my own, dating a German woman, with no one to say anything at all about what I could do. I was told she was the daughter of the mayor of the city of Stuttgart, but we never talked about it. She did have a lot of money and would pick me up anytime of the week, so maybe it was the truth; it didn't matter to me. All I knew was she was beautiful and she wanted me. Although I enjoyed my time with Helga, the romance came to an end in abrupt fashion. Helga simply dropped off the face of the earth. I still wonder whatever happened to her.

19
Strange Sexual Encounter

Even with Helga out of the picture, life as a singer and bassist with the Soul Brothers was hardly dull. One night we were playing at the Fifty Meter Club and this older guy, around 55, came in with his girlfriend. He spoke to Marvin, who came back to the rest of us and said, "This man wants us to go with him after the gig is over." I asked him "For what?" Marvin responded that this man wanted us to have sex with his girlfriend, so he could watch. I said "Not me!" Marvin said he wanted all of us or none. Again, I said, "No!" The German man came up to me and said his friend wanted to have sex with all of us. The young lady was looking at me with a smile on her face, and the man was talking to me in German. So, after the gig, we all went out to this field way out in the country. He had a big black Mercedes, the old kind they use for taxis in Europe. She got in the back seat, and, one by one, pointed to each of us and we got into the back seat, and, well, you know the rest. Each time she finished with one of us she would clean herself up. The strangest part for me was that her boyfriend took a very thin stick and spanked her on the butt, getting her all excited, and then she called on the next person. This went on until we all had sex with her. They thanked us and left. I never saw them again.

20

Marvin:
The Worst Kind of Bully

I continued to sit in with the band on a regular basis, despite the abundance of temptation around me. I remained focused on the music. My passion for music continued to grow and soon the military stepped in to give me my lucky chance to step to the musical forefront. Jeff, the lead singer of the band, was transferred to another base. I capitalized on his rapport with the other band members and became the lead singer of the Five Soul Brothers. I could see right off that I was not going to get along with Marvin, who was a bully and a loudmouth. He always said things like "Don't talk to this woman or that woman; she's mine." The two of us couldn't see eye-to-eye on a lot of things, which led to several arguments and a deteriorating relationship.

The band's bassist, Sergeant Johnson, was shipped out to another base not long after I assumed duties as the lead singer. Marvin approached me and told me I also had to learn to play bass. I suggested we search for a new bass player to maintain the five-man configuration. Marvin won the battle of wills and I became the bass player. Although I did not have a bass to play, he got a guitar and we filed it down so that it became a bass. I did the work and Marvin showed me how. He gave me a stack of records and said, "These are the songs you *gotta* learn." I loved singing so much that I learned how to play and sing at the same time. Marvin became the leader of the band, bullying me the whole time. Once again, there was a bully in my life. I was not a brave person back then and I never learned how to fight. I could talk a good fight, but fist-fighting was not my thing.

Even our gigs were fraught with thick air between Marvin and me. One night he and I got into it at the gig. I don't remember what it was about, but I am pretty sure it was over a girl. He invited me outside. I couldn't let everyone see I was scared so I took him up on his offer, hoping that someone would stop the fight before it started. Thankfully, the sergeant was there to step in and discourage both of us hot-tempered men from going at each other's throats.

Most of the time we argued a lot, but my love for music was so great that I took Marvin's shit and played anyway. Sergeant Johnson was transferred after playing only a couple of shows with us.

The Soul Brothers were invited to tour Germany, playing for the troops. We played behind a four-man group called The Capris for about three months. On this tour the Soul Brothers performed alongside future legends. The first time I saw Rufus Thomas he had a hit song called "Walking the Dog." We did shows with him on some of the bases. It was a great time for me. As always, music would make things all right, even when things seemed out of sorts.

While touring through Germany, as a member of the Soul Brothers, I experienced a very dark moment. This was one of the ugliest events in my personal life, during that time. Marvin and I were driving and saw this young lady hitchhiking. I was at the wheel when Marvin asked me to stop and give her a ride. So, I obliged. We stopped, picked her up, and continued to drive. Marvin and the young lady were talking. We learned she was a nurse, and then Marvin started to ask her personal questions. I asked him why he asked whatever it was he had asked her and he told me to be quiet. They kept on talking and he climbed into the backseat, where they started to kiss. He started to get rough with her and I pulled over and told him to stop. He told me to "Fuck Off" and continued to take advantage of this girl. I was so scared that I did nothing; to this day I think about this. When he finished he asked me if I wanted "some," but I said no. I sat in the backseat with the young lady and told her I was sorry this happened. Marvin repeated over and over that this young lady wanted it. We took her where she wanted to go and left her there. This incident was the lowest point in my military life.

Marvin got shot in his hand, years later, for the doing the same thing he did to that girl in Germany, to a white, American girl, by a man that was not afraid like I was, at the time. From what I was told of the incident, they were at a restaurant called Hy's, on

MacArthur Blvd. in Oakland. Apparently, Marvin was messing with one of *Hamp's* ladies and *Hamp* told him to leave her alone. *Hamp* was a so-called dancer and somewhat of a pimp, notorious in the Oakland Bay Area.

Marvin, the asshole that he was, laughed at *Hamp* and kept after the lady. They got in some heated words and Marvin talked shit like he was going to kick *Hamp's* ass and went after him. This time he was stopped right in his tracks. *Hamp* pulled out a Derringer pistol and shot him in the left arm, his playing arm. I was not there so I can't elaborate much more, but it was the talk of Oakland at the time.

I went back to my job on our base, as a medical records clerk in the dispensary, after we finished the tours on the bases. We continued to play on weekends at the Fifty Meter Club.

21
Margaret

It was during the holidays in 1963 that I met Margaret. She came into the Fifty Meter Club with her sister. She was the most beautiful woman I had ever seen: she had red hair, green eyes, stood about five foot six inches tall and was perfect in all ways, as far as I was concerned. This was one person Marvin was not going to bully me out of. I think he knew Margaret's sister because they started to talk. Margaret was someone I knew I wanted and we started to talk, but she could not speak any English and I did not know German at all. We fell in love from the first time we saw each other. I knew that she was the one for me, my first true love. It was as if God had put her in my life at that moment. Somehow, we got through the first night with sign language and her sister helping us to communicate.

Margaret and I became a couple immediately. Our inability to verbally communicate was a hurdle we easily cleared. Soon things became serious. My life changed forever. We started to date. She was not from a rich family, but I didn't care. Money was not important to me, only her love and being with her. For the rest of the time I was in Germany she was the person in my life. I wrote home telling Mother that I had found the woman of my dreams, the person I wanted to marry. Mother wrote back and said something to the effect that I already had a wife. I wrote back, "No, I don't! Margaret is going to be my wife, no matter what." The letters back and forth soon stopped and I was focused on Margaret. This was the best time of my life. We spent as much time as we could together. I was lost in her love. She was a beautiful, kind, wonderful person. I remember the first time we made love. It was way out in an open field, covered with snow. She was a joy to me; I loved her with all my heart, so what Mother said did not matter at all.

When my entire company was shipped out to Vietnam I went AWOL (Absent without Leave) to be with Margaret. I got a ride on the back of a Moped scooter and all that was on my mind was getting to Margaret. There was a little bed and breakfast in town where Margaret and I often went. The owner did not want us to stay, at first, because we were not married. We told her we were going to get married and move to the U.S., so she let us stay.

For the next year or so she became my world. I met a lot of Margaret's family. Her father was not there, so I was not sure if he had passed away or just left. It was just Margaret, her mother, and her brother. They were very poor and we had to make-do with what was on hand to eat. Margaret's brother and I would hunt for food. They were so poor that we went hunting for pigeons. I had very little money, but whatever I had I gave to them. I stopped writing home as much and spent most of my time with Margaret and her family.

Margaret and I grew deeper in love with each other and soon she had wonderful news for me. One day she told me she was pregnant. I could not have been happier. I knew she was going to be my wife and family, forever. I wrote my mother to tell her Margaret was carrying my child and that I wanted to marry and bring her to the U.S. This was one of the few times my mother did not say a word; she would say things like "We can deal with this when you get home." **I did not know that she had already officiated a fake marriage, using my brother Joe as a stand-in for me and my sister as a witness. This was not legal, of course, but to Mother it was good enough.** Life went on the same for Margaret and me. All I could think about was going home and having a family with Margaret and my first child. I did not know this was not going to happen.

As love and some semblance of a music career were blossoming for me in Germany, Mother was taking dramatic actions back home, rendering me a passive observer to the most important personal decision of my life. As far as I was concerned, Mary was completely out of the picture, as she had been since I left for Germany. Once things got serious with Margaret, I wrote Mary to reiterate in no uncertain terms that the relationship between us was over. Mary had been corresponding with Mother ever since I'd been in Germany and the two women had struck up a rapport. Eventually, Mother sent for Mary and even offered her a place to stay. Mary took my mother up on the offer and she made the cross-continental journey to Oakland, taking up residence with Mother and the rest of the family. I had no idea this was going down. Mother already determined that Mary was going to be my wife.

Mary, initially, got along well with Mother and her light skin all but guaranteed my children would not be cursed with dark skin. Once Mother made the decision on my behalf that I would be wed to Mary, she sent a letter informing me. Mother dismissed my repeated declarations of love for Margaret and proceeded to tell all her friends that Ollan and Mary were husband and wife. It is unclear, beyond her preference for her light skin tone, why Mother took such a liking to Mary.

When I had first met Mary back in Louisiana I sent Mother a picture of her, explaining that I liked her. It was mostly about the sex; I did not want to marry her, and yet I was taught you had to marry the woman you slept with, no matter what. As I said, Grandmother and Mother went crazy over Mary's light skin. That's all they cared about. I assumed that when Mary and Mother began writing back and forth, they got along so well because they were both control freaks. For Mary's part, she was eager to leave the dreary poverty of Louisiana, and the opportunity to head westward could not have come at a better time for her.

The dynamic between Mary and Mother grew stronger soon after Mary took up residence in Mother's house. Once Mary became a part of *Arvanola's* household, she soon grew tired of Mother's need for control. Mary frequently snuck out and became familiar with the GIs in the Bay Area.

In protest to all these developments happening against my will, I stopped sending money back home. I was called into the office of the Post Master not too long after I cut off the money supply. The officer asked me whether it was true that I had stopped sending money home. When I stood by my decision, the officer quickly ended the matter by insisting that I had to send money back home. Mother's interference did not end in my home; it also carried over into my military life. Unbeknownst to me, Mother sent ugly letters to Margaret once I was back home. This was a possibility I did not consider when I used Margaret's address to send correspondences back home. Life with Margaret was an oasis, despite the tumult surrounding my future marital status. I spent the rest of the time I had left in Germany watching Margaret get very pregnant and loving it very much. This was my first child to a beautiful woman that I loved very much. I was demoted by my first sergeant for going off the base without permission.

Leaving the base AWOL for nearly a week left me on shaky ground. The scrutiny made it more difficult for me to get away to see Margaret, but I got creative. I knew I would be in trouble if I left the post, but I left anyway. This time, when I got back, I had to fake sickness so that I would not get into major trouble. So I said someone had given me some drugs. I said I was out and did not know what had happened. They took me to the infirmary and gave me a shot, which I was not expecting, to put me into a deep sleep. This was not good because we had to go out on maneuvers the next day and I was all drugged-up. I had outsmarted myself on this one. When it came time to leave Germany, Margaret and I were not happy about this, yet we knew my departure time would come one day. She would follow me to the States. At least, this was the plan.

Margaret was very pregnant when I left Germany, and I was very happy, because soon she would come to my home in the United States. All I could think about was that my bride-to-be, new baby and I would happily live together, and forget all about Mary and my mother's plan. Finally, the day arrived when I had to go. This was a very sad day for me, Margaret, her mother and brother. It was the beginning of the end of the possibility of ever having a normal life of my own choosing; I never sent for Margaret. From that point on my life was turmoil. I would never be completely happy in love. I would always have a large, empty hole in my soul, and it was all due to my mother and her control over me. Getting on the train to go to the boat, shipping out, Margaret was standing there. My last words to her were "I will send for you," but ultimately they proved false, in spite of all of my best intentions. I thought of nothing on the trip back to the U.S. but Margaret and my new baby.

Margret and
my first son
Johnny.

I did not get
these pictures
until after my
mother and sister
Lynne died.

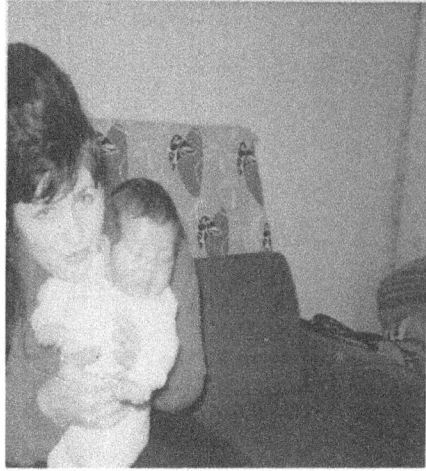

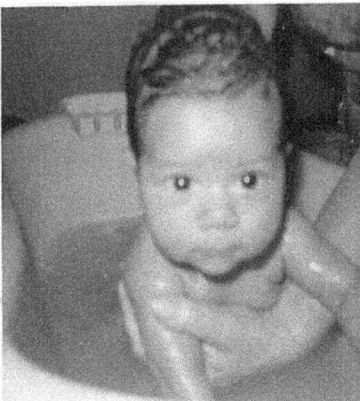

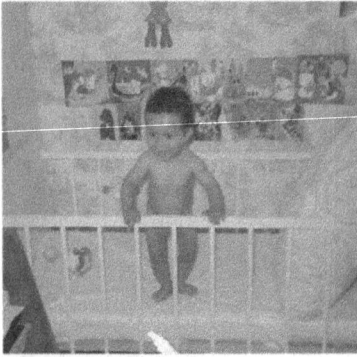

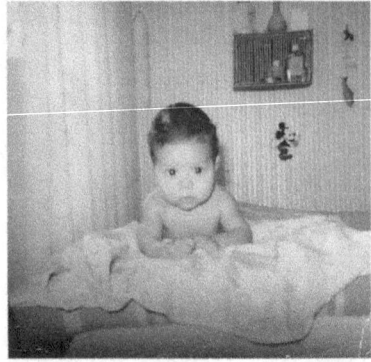

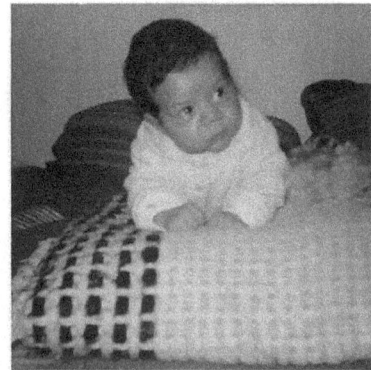

22
Back To Oakland:
"Prisoner of Zenda"

I finally got back to Fort Dix, New Jersey, where I was discharged out of the Army. Then I made my first trip on a commercial airplane to return to California. During the flight, I did not know where the bathroom was. I had to pee and didn't know what to do. So, being taught to "make-do" with what was on hand, I took the airsick bag and used it for a urinal. This did not work out very well; I ended up with pee all over the place. I spent the entire trip wet, unable to move, and very embarrassed. Getting ready to leave the plane, I waited for the person that was sitting next to me to get off first. When we arrived at the airport lobby, I found a bathroom and changed into my street clothes.

My mother was at the airport to meet me and lay down her law. She told me, forcefully, that I was now married to Mary. I told her I wanted Margaret to be my wife, but Mother's words were "You are already married, and that is that." I said that I didn't want Mary at all and that she should send her back to her family. I asked my mother for the money I sent back from Germany. She informed me that the money I sent was to help with my brothers and sisters, not to send for someone we don't know from another country. I did not know what to say. I was back home with no money, a so-called wife I did not want, and my mother telling me how to live my life. I stood there, shaking, because I didn't know what to do.

This was the worst thing that could have happened to me in my life, even more devastating than witnessing Marvin rape that young lady back in Germany. I arrived at Mother's house on Thursday, June 11th, 1964, four days before my 21st birthday. My choices were to get out of the house, with no place to go, or take this person I did not know to Reno and marry her. I seemed to go into a deep fog at this time because I could not believe this was happening. I told Mary I did not want to marry her and it was as though no one was hearing me. She and the family had it all worked out for me.

My brother, Joe, was constantly getting drunk because he had been sleeping with Mary for the last three years, but I did not know it. I kept on repeating that I did not want to get married nor did I want to have any children with Mary, because I had a child on the way and needed to deal with that. Mother pushed this aside and gave me an ultimatum.

The next day, Mary, Lynne, and I were on a Greyhound bus headed to Reno. Mother told us just what to do and the entire way there I was very ugly about the whole thing. I told Mary I did not love her. I said this was not right and she should go home to Louisiana. We got to Reno and my sister, Lynne, did just as Mother told her to do, being the eldest and most controlled by my mother. We went into this church-like place and these two white people, a man and a woman, came to get us. While all this was going on I repeated to Mary, "I don't want to marry you." She kept this blank look on her face, as if I was not there. I was screaming at her, asking her why she wanted to marry me when I didn't love her. She never opened her mouth; she just looked straight ahead. I was also screaming at Lynne. Why was she doing this to me? The whole time we were on the bus I screamed so loudly that other passengers complained, yelling at me to shut up. The bus driver also told me to pipe down or he would put me off the bus. We did the marriage thing and returned home the same day. I would grow accustomed to Mary's blank stare, over time; it was the expression she took on when she wanted to dismiss you.

When we returned home it was time for bed. I reiterated to Mary that I did not want to have any children or to even sleep with her. This latter part did not matter to Mary. The only thing that bothered her was when I said I did not want any children. Then she started to cry. I did not understand then, with all the ugly things I was saying to her, that the only time she felt so hurt to tears was when I said I did not want children with her. In hindsight, I understand why she was crying. Later, I found out Mary was six months pregnant with my brother, Joe's baby, which explains why she needed me to sleep with her. It was so she could attribute paternity to me. The math obviously precluded the possibility of my paternity, yet everyone around me insisted the baby was mine. I took responsibility for this child, partially out of duty but mainly due to my naiveté. DNA testing didn't exist back then so I could not prove anything. I was in a complete fog, by this point.

A lot had transpired while I was overseas. Mary and my sister Lynne had become really close over the past three years. I always wondered why. I found out much later that Lynne had gone to New York and also gotten pregnant while she was there, before returning to Oakland. She married another guy named Clyde and claimed the baby was his. Mary knew all of this, so there was this secret Lynne and Mary shared.

I also found out later that Mother had been receiving letters from Margaret, but not telling me. I would go to work and when I returned home ask if there was any mail for me. I was always told "No." Mother had already gotten the mail, took the letters Margaret had sent, and did not tell me anything. Margaret was not only sending letters to Mother but also pictures of my first child, who was a boy. Meanwhile, I began to worry because I hadn't heard from Margaret, and Mary kept me busy having sex. Like all men, I began thinking with the wrong head, as such, and, being very young, I was doomed. My marriage to Mary was like being in prison, hindering me from acting upon my true love for Margaret and from being a father to my first son, Johnny. I didn't know then that this would haunt me for the rest of my life.

We stayed with my mother for about a month and I got a job at General Motors, in Fremont, California, starting on the night shift. Mother became the worst parent, in all ways. She seemed to turn into a monster after my return from Germany. First, she never told me about my first-born son, and then sent ugly letters to Margaret, for no other reason than to make her feel bad. The worse part of this is that it went on even after my mother's death. The pictures and letters continued to come. Mother had passed them on to Lynne, who also hid them from me. I never saw or read them. Lynne, too, carried this ugly secret to her grave. My sister's son, Jeffrey, brought the pictures to my home one day while we were having band rehearsal. He came by and gave me the pictures, along with some ugly words about my sister having to keep this fucked-up secret all these years. Of course, Mary knew all about it, as did my sister Rose. I was the only one in the dark for over 20 years.

In the midst of all of this domestic turmoil, I stayed close to music. Soon after I returned to the US from Germany, I tried out for a contest held at the Bo Peep Club in San Francisco. It was my first encounter with Sly Stone. When I arrived there was this guy I did not know giving orders and pushing people around. I said I wanted to try out and he told me to "Get the fuck off the stage. Tryouts are over." I had just gotten out of the service and was not about to take orders from some clown. We had a few ugly words and I said to him, "I was told to come try out and that is what I am going to do." He barked at me that this was his show and that I was not going to do shit. I said, "Fuck you!" and we got into a bit of a scuffle. It was broken up and I never did get my chance to try out. Sly and I haven't spoken ever since, other than small talk. He played Natural Four records on his radio show once we hit, but we never said more than "What's up?" to each other after that, even when we were in the same room together.

I adopted a cavalier attitude toward the wedding vows I was forced into. I sought relationships outside of the marriage almost immediately, and continued to do so over the course of my 24-year marriage to Mary. My first encounter was with one of Mary's sisters. Mary and I had moved out of Mother's house, and into a house in the Oakland Hills. Her sister came to live with us to help Mary with the new baby. Mary went to the hospital one morning, and they kept her. Her sister left Mary at the hospital that day and came back to the house. That night, when I got ready to go to bed, the sister came into our room and got in bed with me. At first I could not believe what was happening, and then I understood. Mary was in the hospital for three days and that sister slept with me all three days. When Mary got home, she stopped as quickly as she had started, like nothing happened. We moved forward as though nothing happened.

I had to get a job to support this woman and this child, yet the entire time my brother was saying that it was his child. Joe and I fought over everything since we were children, and he was such a liar I did not believe him. When I asked Mary about it she would say Joe was lying, that this was my child. For years, I really did believe Monique was my biological daughter.

70

Things came to a head between Joe and me one evening. Right after I returned home from work we had a real bad fight over Mary. He came to my house and started saying things I thought were crazy, at the time. He told me that Mary's baby was his and I said he was a liar. I told him to leave my house and he said "Fuck You!" Then the fight started. Mary stood there saying nothing at all, just looking. We took it outside. I was faster than he was, so he chased me as I ran back into the house and locked the door. "I'll call the cops if you don't go away!" I yelled. We did not talk for a long time after that.

Over the next several years Mary's other sisters came to live with us, making things even crazier for me. We moved up into the hills of Oakland, renting a flea-infested house. Mary's sister, Emily, who was pregnant at the time, came to live with us when we lived on Michigan Street. Mary was also pregnant with my son, Mark. This was a very strange time for me because everything that was happening was based around the fact that Mary had my brother's first child.

I was sure Margaret had moved on after one year or so, believing that I would never come back. And I never did. I went deeper and deeper into my shell, depressed that I couldn't be with the woman I loved. During this time I kept on singing, never forgetting I had a child. But what could I do? I had no way of contacting the child or his mother. This was a time of transition. I didn't even try to hide that I was having affairs. I came home late, and sometimes not at all. I had a woman to visit all the time, and it was not always about having sex. Sometimes I just needed to talk to someone.

Mary was not the sharpest knife in the drawer. I never remember Mary going to vote or taking a stand about anything at all. She did not read the newspaper or talk about anything that was important. Although my mother was insane, if not clinically, she read a lot, even though I did not. I listened to all that she said and was able to pick up the parts that worked for me, and use them in my best interest. The only thing that the Guidry family liked to do was play card games, particularly Bid Whist. I am sure I would not have

71

looked outside my marriage if I had been with Margaret; she was all I needed. But I was stuck with someone I did not love, trying to raise a family that was built on lies and deception. Losing a wonderful woman, the mother of my first child, took a deep toll on me, and the way I would turn out in my adult life.

The thing that was most calming about Margaret was her kind words all the time when we were together. With all of Mary's un-redeeming qualities, the one that unnerved me the most was her glaring inability to cook. Her chicken tasted like wood. I suffered a seemingly terminal case of indigestion and headaches behind her cooking. I was constantly taking Ex-Lax, and Excedrin for headaches. Mary was nonchalant about the whole situation; she was also having affairs right under my nose. Those included sleeping with several of my so-called friends, one in particular from whom she contracted a bad case of crabs and brought it straight home to me. I guess she thought "I'll keep this nigger happy by giving him some from time to time." And Mary did just that for 20 years. I even went as far as to ask her to dye her hair red, like Margaret's. Going with the flow, Mary conceded to my request.

We moved to an apartment in Oakland, on 81st Avenue. While I was at work, Joe went to my house and continued to sleep with Mary. When I called to check on things at home he was there "just visiting," he said. The whispers of an illicit relationship between Joseph and Mary suddenly grew louder in my ear each night I phoned home and heard Joseph in the background. I would ask why Joe was there and Mary gave me some bullshit answer. We moved to another house in Oakland and this was when Mary's sisters began coming to Oakland to stay with us again. The relationship between Mary and Joseph was, in retrospect, bound to happen.

I was uncertain of how I was going to deal with this prison-like marriage, but time didn't wait for me to figure it out. On February 28, 1966, Mary gave birth to Monique James. Questions of paternity flooded my mind with even more prevalence, since the baby, Monique, looked very similar to Joseph. Suddenly, the "crazy" things that Joseph said in the heat of our fight seemed plausible. I dismissed his doubts and eased into fatherhood, working steadily at the GM plant and bringing home a decent pay to my new family.

Once Monique was born we were like a model couple, from the outside, especially, compared to our upstairs neighbors, another young couple who were always fighting. The husband beat his wife. I was never into fighting. After the first year and a half into our marriage, I went on autopilot, oblivious to everyone. Mary, with her quiet demeanor, portrayed the dutiful young wife and mother who kept a good home for her hard-working husband, while I mastered the role of provider and father. I became a master at deception. No one would have ever caught on that this young married couple established their lives together on a crumbling foundation, with a lingering question of paternity hanging over their heads.

Marriage Service

This Certifies that

of _Alan Christopher Bell James_
and _Oakland, Calif._
of _Mary Louise Guidry_
Lake Charles, Louisiana

were by me united in the bonds of

Marriage

at _Oakland California_

on the _23_ day of _July_
in the year of our Lord Nineteen Hundred
and _Sixty three_
conformably to the ordinance of God and
the Laws of the State.

Granalo C. Jordan
Licensed.   **Minister**

Witnesses _Lynne T. Dufait_
Joseph D. Bell
License _No. 604 Universal_

Then the Minister, calling the Man by his Christian name, shall say:

Allan Christopher James

wilt thou have this Woman to be thy wife, and wilt thou pledge thy troth to her, in all love and honor, in all duty and service, in all faith and tenderness, to live with her, and cherish her, according to the ordinance of God, in the holy bond of marriage?

The Man shall answer:

I will.

Then the Minister, calling the Woman by her Christian name, shall say:

Mary Louise Guidry

wilt thou have this Man to be thy husband, and wilt thou pledge thy troth to him, in all love and honor, in all duty and service, in all faith and tenderness, to live with him, and cherish him, according to the ordinance of God, in the holy bond of marriage?

The Woman shall answer:

I will.

I Mary Louise Guidry will

76

Then the Minister may say:

Who giveth this Woman to be married to this Man? I *Joseph James*

Then the Father, or Guardian, or Friend, of the Woman shall put her right hand in the hand of the Minister, who shall cause the Man with his right hand to take the Woman by her right hand and to say after the Minister as follows:

I *Alfred Christopher* take thee, *Ollan Christopher,* To be my wedded wife; And I do promise and covenant; Before God and these witnesses; To be thy loving and faithful husband; In plenty and in want; In joy and in sorrow; In sickness and in health; As long as we both shall live.

Then shall they loose their hands; and the Woman, with her right hand taking the Man by his right hand, shall likewise say after the Minister:

I *Mary Louise Gindry*,
take thee, *Allan Christopher*,
To be my wedded husband; And I do promise and covenant; Before God and these
witnesses; To be thy loving and faithful wife;
In plenty and in want; In joy and in sorrow;
In sickness and in health; As long as we both
shall live.

*Then if a ring be provided, it shall be given to
the Minister, who shall return it to the
Man, who shall then put it upon the fourth
finger of the Woman's left hand, saying
after the Minister:*

This ring I give thee; In token and pledge;
Of our constant faith; And abiding love.

Or,

With this ring I thee wed; In the name of
the Father; And of the Son; And of the Holy
Spirit. Amen.

Before giving the ring, the Minister may say:

Bless, O Lord, this ring, that he who gives
it and she who wears it may abide in Thy

Our Father, who art in heaven; Hallowed be Thy name. Thy kingdom come. Thy will be done; On earth as it is in heaven. Give us this day our daily bread. And forgive us our debts; As we forgive our debtors. And lead us not into temptation; But deliver us from evil; For Thine is the kingdom, and the power, and the glory, for ever. Amen.

Then shall the Minister say unto all who are present:

By the authority committed unto me as a Minister of the Church of Christ, I declare that *Allan Christopher James* and *Mary Louise Guidry* are now Husband and Wife, according to the ordinance of God, and the law of the State: in the name of the Father, and of the Son, and of the Holy Spirit. Amen.

Then, causing the Husband and Wife to join their right hands, the Minister shall say:

Mary did not waste any time getting pregnant again, and 11 months later Mark was born. I often slipped up and called her Margaret, which she obviously did not like. But I had been accustomed to saying Margaret's name every day for the past two years, so it was a habit I did not want to break. My plan was to save enough money to leave, no matter what. I had not received any letters from Margaret, so I did not know what to think. By this time, I was working at GM and dealing with a baby I thought was mine, with another one on the way.

I got into the routine of fatherhood and being a husband. My dream of having Margaret as my wife was fading more and more each day. My respect for Mary was nonexistent, and my mother was still sticking her nose heavily into my life, one way or another. Usually, it was like a bad dream that I couldn't wake up from.

I was losing my first child. I say *first child* because I did not know whether it was a boy or a girl, at the time. I was working every day, and it felt like I was just going through the motions. Days turned into weeks, weeks into months, and months into years. I soon became resigned to my circumstance, letting each day go by. I dealt only in the moment. My mother remained in close contact with us, primarily through Mary. She was still manipulating my life and I had no idea. After a while, Mary made sure I had sex as often as I wanted, never doing anything special, just keeping me tied to her through sex. Then we started using drugs together. At first it was weed, then cocaine. This went off and on for about five years. Even during this time, Margaret was still in the forefront of my mind, but Mary did not care. She was fine with whatever I wanted to do, as long as she kept safe her secret about Monique.

23
Never Quit Singing

Escaping to the nightclubs in Oakland, my home life was in shambles. My favorite spot was Al's House of Smiles on East 14th Street, now International Boulevard. Al's was a cocktail lounge with a tiny bandstand raised high above the audience. I first sang there with a band called Eugene Blacknell and The New Breed. Eugene was a gifted guitar player who died very young from a heart attack. With his blues-infused guitar style, Eugene was very popular on the Bay Area funk scene. Each Sunday there was a contest so I went down and signed up. Winning the first time I tried out, I got to sing the next weekend and get paid. I continued working steadily at the GM plant.

Natural Four Going to Top in High Gear

The original Natural Four
Allen Richardson, Chris James (aka Ollan Bell), John January,
Alfred Milton Bowden

Alfred Milton "Punkin" Bowden and I met six months after I got the job at the General Motors plant, between 1966 and 1967. Some of the guys had heard me singing around the plant, as I worked on the truck line, and said there was another guy who sang in a group who I should meet. *Punkin* told me he and his group were looking for a lead singer and first tenor and he asked me if I would like to try out. At the time they were called The Dynamic Dimensions. I went to the first audition, met the guys, and they liked me very much. I was then using my first name, Ollan, and the last name Mother had given me, so I was called Ollan James. We were at practice one day and this clown who called himself "Terrible" Tom, *Punkin's* brother, said, "What kind of name is Ollan, nigga? You need to change your name to something cool." I told him my real name was Ollan Christopher Bell-James, still using the last name of James, not thinking about being true to myself. "Terrible" Tom said "Look, nigga, you gonna change your name to Chris James." I agreed. The name had a ring to it. Henceforth, this became the name that would follow me for most of my professional life.

The members of the Dynamic Dimensions, soon to be renamed the Natural Four, were essentially a group of working guys who were serious about music, to varying degrees. *Punkin,* the leader of the group, was ironically the least qualified as a vocalist, perhaps the worst first tenor I've ever worked with. Nevertheless, the brother had a good stage personality. Allen Richardson was the laid-back and suave one. He had a good job as a longshoreman and music was just a hobby for him. John January was a very mellow brother and a notably good vocalist. He was working as a janitor, at the time, for the Berkeley School District. Like Allen, music was just a hobby for him.

We ultimately had to change the name of the group from the Dynamic Dimensions, because it sounded too much like the rising pop-soul group Friends of Distinction. Back in the 1960's, "the natural" was the way to go for Black people. If you had a big *Afro* you were very hip. The bigger the *fro* the more attention you got. There were shops that specialized in *Afro* wigs, so we were given those to wear. Because I did not have a very thick head of hair, I was one of the first people to wear a wig in the group. John January was also given a wig. Allen did not need one since he had the kind of hair that people called "good hair," the kind that did not need a "permanent." *Punkin* also had a very full head of hair, so he did not need a wig at all. We decided to rename the group the Natural Four,

82

to capitalize on the popularity of *Afros*, and to describe our hairstyles.

We practiced a lot and began doing a few shows around the Bay Area. We were the new kids on the block. There was a group called the Ballads that was popular at the time, so we had to work hard to get to the top. The Ballads, consisting of Nathan Robertson, Jon Foster, Rico Thompson, and Lesley LaPalma had been a popular fixture on the Bay Area soul scene since 1961. The group enjoyed a top ten R&B hit in the summer of 1968, with the soulful slow jam "God Bless Our Love." They had a few more local hits out and were also pimps, to help when gigs were slow.

We performed a lot of gigs in town at clubs like the Sportsman, the Showcase, and the Centennial. Things got even better for the group. We started getting a lot of calls to do shows in San Francisco and around the Bay Area. Our first managers were Billy Barnes and Fred and Jay Ivey. Billy worked with some other brothers who ran a production company, so we traveled around the surrounding towns doing shows featuring all of the big local groups in the area. There were groups like the Hartfield Brothers, the Uptights, Johnny Tolbert and De-Thangs, and the Whispers, just to name a few. At around the same time, we landed a gig at a place called The Dragon A' Go-Go (1965-68), a basement club previously called the Lion's Den, in San Francisco. It was located in Chinatown's underground, at 49 Wentworth Alley. This is where we met our second manager, Louis Chin, owner of the club and a partner with Don Cornelius' Soul Train. We performed there six nights a week, for about six months. We worked at the Dragon A' Go-Go with a crack band called the LBJs. We played there so often and Louis liked us so much that he also wanted to manage us. He took us out and bought us our first tailor-made suits, which were green pinstripe. I was still working at the GM plant. Word got out about the club and all the other groups started to ease in on what had been a place for us to get our skills together.

It was an exciting time for Black music in Oakland, when we were starting out. A who's-who of artists came through the Bay Area in that era. The Temptations, John Lee Hooker, James Brown, Gladys Night and The Pips, Etta James, the Four Tops, the Mad

Lads, the Spinners, Sly and the Family Stone; it was a musical buffet. Sly was a DJ on KDIA 1310 radio, which was the biggest black radio station in the Bay Area. It's now a Christian radio station. Most of the top groups that came from the East Bay played the Oakland Auditorium, the biggest place to gig back then. We played at all the best clubs in the East Bay, places like the Showcase and the Sportsman. We also traveled to Seattle a lot, which was a big deal for us.

Many industry players saw a chance to make money with the Natural Four. We were working with people like Lu Vason, a local promoter, and Willie Hoskins, who was a mediocre producer from Mississippi. Hoskins, who I refer to as "The Thief," had come to Oakland in the late 60's and opened up a rehearsal studio on Telegraph Avenue called Boola Boola Records. Jay and Fred Ivey, from Atlanta, were very slick in the ways of promoting young local unknown acts like the Natural Four. The Ivey brothers handled us as a vocal group while Lu Vason booked us. From 1968 to 1970 we worked a lot. We played schools and the bowling alley in Oakland, while also working at individual jobs. We did shows around the San Francisco Bay Area, Seattle, Denver, and Texas. During our very long lay-off, from 1970 to 1972, I worked as an MC at a place in Richmond called the McKesmo Club. Around this time, the Whispers came to town.

We recorded our first songs at Sierra Sounds Studio in Berkeley, California. The first song was "I Thought You Were Mine." It was recorded with John January, Allen Richardson, and Alford "Punkin" Milton Bowden. The songwriter was a singer named Lonnie Cook. We practiced at Willie Hoskins' studio, sometimes six nights a week, drinking cheap wine and smoking weed all night. The song caught the ear of ABC Records and we landed our first record contract. Or, rather, Willie Hoskins landed his record contract. "I Thought You Were Mine" blew up on the local scene and kept us working. Capitalizing on the momentum of our local hit, we went back into the studio and recorded songs for our first LP, *Good Vibes*. We started to get a lot of airplay around the Bay Area, and in places like Seattle and Denver. Things went smoothly for us for a few months. Although we worked the regional scene, most of the time we stayed in Oakland and San Francisco.

84

We started getting a lot of gigs and had a song on the radio, so the girls were running after us like we were the Beatles. We worked with groups like Earth Wind & Fire, when Sherry Scott was singing with them. I remember Lenny Williams was an opening act for us. We performed with him at a high school show promoted by Billy Barns, in Vallejo. He was scared to death, and we talked backstage. I told him not to worry it was nothing but a gig. Not long after that he got his career-making chance to audition for Tower of Power.

We hit pay dirt in 1969 with the release of "Why Should We Stop Now," a real turning point for the Natural Four. Willie Hoskins was riding high on our ABC Records deal. We were naive to the business details, so Willie handled all of the contracts and told us that everything was good, but, of course, it was not. That advance money he received, approximately $150,000, was generated from the momentum of our hit single, yet the Natural Four did not see a penny of it. He put contracts in front of us and assured us, "Don't worry, I will take care of everything." He sure did. He spent the money on a new car, a house, and producing records on other acts in the Bay Area, like the Ballads, the Hartfield Brothers, and the Whispers, while the Natural Four got nothing. By the time we discovered Willie mishandled our earnings it was too late to do anything; he had already skipped town and moved to Los Angeles.

We were preparing to travel to a show in Seattle when Allen's wife was involved in a serious car accident, which caused major problems for the group. Allen, understandably, did not want to take the trip, and neither did John. As the old adage goes "The show must go on," so we had to find two new singers. This was another major turning point for the group. Frantic to find replacements for Allen and John, I went to the Showcase on a Thursday, when the club hosted a talent night. I did this for about two weeks, then one Thursday evening I went in and there was this brother named "Stunning" Steve Striplin who got up and sang. He sounded great and I asked him if he would like to try out for my group. He agreed and did well, becoming a member of the Natural Four.

Simultaneously, Willie Hoskins and Lu Vason were also looking for singers because we had a show coming up that Lu had booked, and we needed to find a fourth member soon. Willie called me up one evening and said "I have another singer for you." I said, "Fine, when can we hear him?" Willie said "Tonight." We had practice and Delmos Whitley came to sing with us. After hearing him we said, "Okay he is in." I did not know at the time that Delmos had just gotten out of jail for his participation in a car theft ring. Neither Willie nor Lu told us until after we had been practicing for the show and had it all together. I remember Willie saying something about "a minor charge" and that it was "okay with his parole officer for Delmos to go out of the state."

The record deal happened before Darryl, Steve, and Delmos began singing with the group. Willie kept this quiet, never telling us he had received that advance of $150.000 for signing us. He told us to sign on the dotted line, and that he would take care of everything else. Like most of the groups back then, we did not know the business and people like Willie Hoskins took advantage of that fact. Of the groups Willie produced, the Natural Four were the last to move forward, mainly because of our change in lineup. When John January and Allen quit things changed a lot. I also didn't know at the time that Delmos would be the reason for the group's breakup.

Around that time we were in touch with a producer named Ron Carson. Ron told me that they were going to take me to Los Angeles to record a song titled, "I Only Meant To Wet My Feet." I was excited. Unbeknownst to me, Ron was using me as bait to get the Whispers to sign with this guy by the name of Dick Griffey. I recorded the lead vocals in Los Angeles and the rest of the Natural Four recorded the background vocals at Sierra Sounds Recording Studio in Berkeley. Early one morning I got a call from Steve Striplin, excited because the song was now on the radio being played on KDIA, as well as KSOL. These were the two main Black radio stations in Northern California. But to my horror and surprise, when I heard the song on the radio, it was not me singing. The Whispers were singing it exactly the way I had sung it. That's when I found out that my recording was simply a demo. The whole idea of them taking me to LA and recording me was to induce the Whispers to sign a contract. The manipulation that was all too familiar in my personal life was now being mirrored in my music career.

24

The Second Stage of the Natural Four: Chris, *Punkin*, Steve, and Delmos

For the next couple of years, with this second edition of the group, we continued to play shows in the San Francisco Bay Area, Texas, Denver, and Seattle. In Texas we performed at the Cinder Club, on the outskirts of Houston, one of many clubs owned by local legend Ray Barnett. We were on the bill with Leroy Daniels and Lawanda Page, actors from the TV show *Sanford and Son*. I remember this place very well because the stage rose up from the middle of the floor. The show was not a success; for some reason or another not too many people showed up. The owner of the club stiffed us for our money and we got stuck in a hotel we could not pay for. They would not let us leave if we did not pay. *Punkin* was the de facto leader of the group at the time. He explained to the hotel manager that it would be better for us to leave, and then we could send the money back to him, but the hotel manager could not see it that way. We must have stayed for a week and a half before the clown realized it was better to let us go, and hope we'd pay the money, than to have us there staying for free and taking rooms from paying customers, even though they stopped all service to our rooms. We met some ladies there, very fat ladies, who kept us well-fed and cleaned our clothes. Naturally, they wanted something in return. I refused to partake in the personal side, so I was left out of the cleaning of the clothes part of things.

While we were in Dallas, Texas, performing at another club, we met some local cats and hung out with them for a while. They asked us if we knew what "robo*"* was, and if we had tried it. Of course, we said "No." They said everybody does "robo" and, like idiots, we asked them to let us try it, which was a big mistake. Back then, smoking weed was about the most any of us was doing. This was in the late 60's. *Punkin* was selling weed, so we always had some around to smoke. Later that day, these guys brought some "robo" for us to try. It turned out that "robo" was a street term for Robitussin cough syrup. These guys were using it to get high because weed wasn't as readily available.

As my family life became more complex, the Natural Four had acquired a following in various cities around the country. We would travel to perform in the hot clubs of the era. When we were in Detroit playing at the legendary Twenty Grand, Steve met a lady and went to her house with Delmos. They were kicking it with these two ladies when one of their husbands found out and went there with his brother to confront them. The two brothers came into the apartment with guns ready to shoot somebody. Luckily, someone saw them and called the police. Steve and Delmos were able to get away from the apartment without any more problems. Later on, at the club, we heard that two men were looking for them, planning to shoot them in the club. That never happened but we got the hell out of town as soon as the gig was over!

Delmos' criminal nature began to have an impact on the group almost as soon as he joined. While we were touring Canada and the United States, we noticed a very large white man who followed us for a month or two as we toured Canada and the U.S. Each time we played at a club we saw this same man, sometimes with one or two others like him. We assumed they were just avid fans but we found out later that they were police, staking out Delmos for a burglary he had committed. In spite of his legal troubles, we always took him back because he was the lead vocalist on what turned out to be our biggest hit, "Can This Be Real." The song was not a hit because of his lead singing, necessarily, but it was the hook that had everyone singing along with us.

Upon returning home from this one trip to Denver, after playing a gig at the Shapes Club, we stopped in Elko, Nevada. It had to be around 1969 or '70 when we stopped at this gas station and filled up. There were two cars; one had a trailer on the back carrying all of our gear. We went inside to use the bathroom. The station attendant went out to pump the gas and there was a countertop stand with a lot of key chains on it, with dollar coins on them. We were looking at them and took a few, about five dollars' worth. This was one of the first times in my life I took something that I did not pay for, and it became a nightmare. We left the gas station, not thinking anything would happen, on our merry way.

We drove about 200 miles, and just before we got to the California-Nevada border the police came down hard on us. They had followed us, waved to us like nothing was wrong, and as we got to the border they pulled us over. It seemed like a joke, at first, but they shined their flashlights in our faces, saying thing like "Get out of the car and lay on the ground." I said, "Please cut this out and let us drive on." I was surprised it was not a joke. They made us get out of the cars. There were about 13 of us spread out on the ground, with their guns aimed at us. They handcuffed us, put us in cars, and drove us to a police station far from where we were stopped. The place smelled awful and was full of drunken Mexicans. We spent the night there and the next morning they flew us back to Elko to stand trial. The worst part of the flight was we were handcuffed and the plane was a little Piper Cub. Also, no one knew where we were, so anything could have happened to us and we would have been "history." The ordeal wound up being a case of mistaken identity. There was a group of guys wanted for robbing a casino, and the police thought it was us. The gas station attendant lied and told the police that we had taken 30 dollars' worth of coins. This was enough for them to hold us. The trial was the next day, on a Saturday, when we were given about a week's jail time as punishment.

Bruno, our bass player, had no children so he took the rap for all of us. We were housed in separate cells while in jail, and I was put in a cell with a white boy who liked to intimidate people. Bullies seemed to gravitate toward me! He woke up every morning and did pull-ups, so, of course, I did pull-ups too. This went on most of the time I was in the cell with this clown. At the time, we were wearing processed hair and so my head was looking pretty bad after two days with no touch-up. My hair was long. The white boy would part his hair in the morning and then start doing his pull-ups. So, I did the same. For whatever reason, my strategy worked. He left me alone.

You would think the story ends there, right? Wrong. It did not end after we were let out since we were told to come back later to retrieve Bruno. If we did not pick him up at a certain time he would be arrested again and charged with vagrancy. I was the one who had to go back to Elko and get him, so I decided to take my imposing Doberman pinscher dog, just in case. I had a convertible and drove with the top down most of the way back to Elko. The dog got sick in the car along the way but we made it just in time before they would have put Bruno back in jail. I drove all the way back with a brother who had not had a bath since soap was discovered and a sick dog, all because we took a few five-dollar coins. How's that for poetic justice? The sad part of this was that Bruno died of an overdose, several years later.

In 1973-74 we went to Detroit and did a show at a club called Mr. G's, bringing along a so-called bodyguard whose name was Dennis Allen. He was a big guy, standing about six feet five inches tall. He was a friend of Delmos and Darryl. Dennis would go places with us in the Bay Area and on short tour runs out of town. This was the first time we took him so far out of town. He carried a firearm, and told us that he had a permit to carry it outside of California. As far as I was concerned, everything was good. When we got to the city for the gig, there was a problem. I had the contract, which stated we would perform just two shows. We were all at the hotel, so I sent the band to set up for the show later that night. About 45 minutes later we got a call at the hotel room; it was the bandleader telling me that the owner of the club insisted we play for a fashion show in addition to the two shows set forth in the contract. I told him that since it was not in the contract then we would not play the fashion show unless we were paid an additional fee. About 15 minutes later they called again and the club owner, Mr. G, held firm, saying we would play the fashion show, so I said "I'll be right there."

I got dressed and headed to the club, and when I arrived the club owner was sitting at the bar. We exchanged words and I explained to him that what was written in the contract is what we would do and nothing else. The discussion became a bit heated and he said "Let's go into my office, so we can talk in private." I said "Fine," as the owner, the union representatives, and I went into his office to continue the conversation. Mr. G kept on saying that we would play, and I said we would not. This exchange went on for about five or six minutes until he brandished a gun and said, "If you don't play, I will blow your muthafuckin' brains out." I looked at him and laughed. At this point, the union representative said, "Chris, he is not playing; he will shoot you and get away with it."

I looked into the eyes of this fool. He would have surely killed me and gotten away with it, so I went back out to the band. When I approached they asked, "What's up?" I said, "Shut up and just play. Don't say anything, just play." I went back to the hotel and told Dennis, "Come on, we are going back to the club, this fool pulled a gun on me." Our so-called bodyguard retrieved his gun and together we went back to the club. Before we got there, though, I called the cops, not knowing Mr. G had them in his back pocket. When we arrived at the club Dennis had his gun in his pocket. We walked up to the bar and I said "Dennis, this is the man who pulled the gun on me." About this time the police walked in and the owner said, "That man has a gun." I was confident that Dennis would show them his permit to carry, but that wasn't the case. He had none. They hauled Dennis' ass off to jail, and he spent six months there. While doing his time in Detroit he contracted some kind of illness. To this day, he hates me over this incident. In the end, we wound up doing the fashion show and I was the bad guy.

There were a few successes for the Natural Four. Our first TV show appearance was *the Midnight Special.* We were very excited. In our dressing room getting ready for the show, we heard a lot of commotion and loud talking in the hall. We went to check out what was going on and discovered it was Curtis Mayfield and Wilson Pickett, arguing over something. Not wanting to ruin our big debut, we kept out of it. Suddenly, Curtis' manager burst into our dressing room and informed us that the show was not going on. We were shocked! Marv Stuart explained to us that Wilson and Curtis had gotten into a serious fight about who was going to headline the show. Wilson had apparently called Curtis a "monkey," and Curtis refused to do the show with him at all. We were disappointed; here was our introduction to the mainstream music scene. The guys asked me to convince Curtis to please let us do the show. If you remember that episode, which aired September 14, 1973, Curtis comes out and says that there is only one guest on the show. He went on to introduce us to whoever was watching Midnight Special that night!

We also appeared on *Soul Train, Don Kirshner's Rock Concert,* and the *Wolf-Man Jack Show.* We were also lucky enough to play the famed Apollo Theater in New York. We also played the Chicago Amphitheater. When we first did the Apollo, in Harlem, we thought we were so great, and that we were the kings of the show, so we went to the top floor. We were on the bill with New Birth, Curtis Mayfield, and a group called New York City and the Impressions. We found out, after the second show of the day, that climbing the stairs for three shows was not the best thing in the world. The second time we played the Apollo we were with the Friends of Distinction, the Impressions, Curtis Mayfield, the famed Parliament-Funkadelic, my son Mark Anthony and several others. A friend named Jodie and I had gone to junior college together and liked to hang out, and he became a flight engineer for one of the top airlines in the U.S.. This was also around the time when cocaine became the new designer drug in America.

It seemed like everyone had some sort of tool to snort cocaine. I was no different; I wore a little spoon on a silver chain around my neck. The show was over and I had put my son Mark to bed in my room upstairs. I was about to go out to get a drink and find a lovely lady that might want to spend the night with me. It was, after all, my birthday. Everyone said "Come on, Chris, we are having a party for you, man, in the other room!" When I got to the room it was completely dark. I flipped on the lights and to my surprise there was Jodie with five beautiful, young, ladies. They were nude, sitting in a circle on the floor, with a bowl of cocaine in front of them. It does not take a genius to figure out what was going to happen next. We stayed up all night, going to bed about one o'clock the next day. I had to make sure Mark was fed and let him watch TV, while I slept for a while and got ready for the show. Other than that wonderful night, New York was mostly uneventful.

But playing the Apollo was the highlight of my stay there. We did all the things everyone did when you had a hit record back in the day: visit record stores, sign autographs, kiss the ladies, and so on. I met a lady named Bernadette, from New York, who was quite beautiful. We had a short but wonderful relationship. I will never forget her because she wore very thick glasses, and was still beautiful with a wonderful personality.

We went back to New York a few times and played a place called Leviticus, an upscale nightclub where all the stars went, before and after hours. One night in particular Teddy Pendergrass was in the club. Like everyone, I liked the way he sang and asked him to come on up and sing with us, but he was not so happy about this, and kept saying no. I kept egging him on until he sang a few bars of whatever song we were singing at the time. After our show, we were hanging out with everyone when Teddy came up to me and said "Muthafucka, don't ever do that shit to me again, or I will whip yo ass." I responded by saying, "You and what army, muthafucka?" We gave each other a few ugly looks and moved on, never to speak to one another again. Several months later, Teddy was in an accident that left him paralyzed from the waist downward. The fact that he was in the vehicle with a transvestite during the accident, was quite a story on the chitlin' circuit at the time.

Mr. Kelley's was a club in the heart of downtown Chicago, near the river. We were booked there for about a week, through Marv Stuart and Curtis Mayfield's Curtom Records. When we arrived, on that first day, things were a little strange. The Natural Four appeared on stage a little late, having come, like most musicians, through the front door of the club. We were directed to go upstairs to the dressing room, and did not know that the owner of the club had called Marv Stuart, complaining that we came through the front door while some customers were eating. I got the call on the phone in the club and Marv was talking a lot of trash, saying we could not come in late, and, most of all, we could not go in through the front door. Don Cornelius was in the club this night, as was Sandy Baron, a popular comedian of the era. As the evening went on, we were getting a lot of shit from the waiters and waitresses calling us "nigger" as they passed us in the hall, before we got ready to go on stage.

We all became fed up, so the next night we waited as they passed through the swinging doors with their trays of food. We put our feet in front of the door, causing several of them to spill trays of food all over the floor. This did not go over very well with the owner, but they could not prove we did it intentionally. The tensions were high for the remainder of our residency at the club.

Another memorable brush with the law came when my wife, Mary, decided to sign up for welfare. I was working part-time, doing odd jobs, and gigging with the group on and off. Mary wanted

93

to get food stamps to keep a steady flow of income. However, she was also working at the Laundromat, in Berkeley. After six months, I told her she should stop collecting the food stamps because it was against the law. But my words fell on deaf ears. One day we received a letter from the District Attorney, stating we had committed fraud and for us to come in immediately, or they would send the police for us. We went downtown to the District Attorney's office where we were told we had to appear in court, were being charged with fraud and had to go to jail.

Mary and I were each supposed to serve four days and pay back the money we had received from the value of the food stamps, as restitution. Like a good husband, I decided to do all of the eight days. How dumb could I have been? I should have let her do her four days and I do mine. While I was in jail, Santa Rita, to be exact, some of the prisoners knew that I sang with the Natural Four. This one very large brother says to me "Motherfucker, don't you sing with the Natural Four?" I replied, "Yes, why?" He then said, "Sing some Stevie Wonder songs, nigga!" I told him I was not going to sing shit. He replied that if I didn't sing, he and his partners were going to whip my ass, again with the bullying. So, I said, "Fuck it!" and started singing Stevie Wonder until they all went to sleep. After that, I had no problems with anyone. Once again, my music saved my ass.

Funny side-story: in Santa Rita I was given a job to trim a rosebush. When I first started trimming the bush it was about five feet eight inches tall. At the end of the eight days that rose bush was about a one foot tall. At that point, the guards asked if I was crazy. I said, "You told me to trim it and I did."

25
Paula

During a gig at the Dragon A' Go-Go I met one of the most memorable women in my life. The Natural Four were performing there in 1966-67 when Paula, a very tall, beautiful, blonde, young lady came into the club and sat in the front row. When we hit the stage we all noticed her. I was still married to Mary. Paula looked at me straight in my eyes and I knew she wanted to talk to me. All the wives were at the club, also, so it was a bit tricky. She sat there at the end of the show and I went up to her and said hello. We talked and discreetly exchanged numbers.

It was not long before I was spending time at Paula's. I could relax there, watch a fight, have a beer and some interesting conversation. I soon learned that she was a virgin, so our first encounter together was an experience. We saw each other for over 20 years. She would come to visit me in Oakland when she was not on the road with the Ice Capades. One day, she informed me that she was going on a road trip and would not be back for a while. She left town to tour quite often, so there was nothing unusual about this particular trip.

I hadn't heard from her for about a year when she contacted me to let me know she was back in town and wanted to see me. I was glad. 28 years later, I found out Paula had gotten pregnant and gone off and given our daughter away to the Wilson family. We continued to see each other for years after this but it became less and less about sex. We became more like very close friends, talking and having a drink together every now and then. Paula was another great oasis from home. Mary was happy to sit around playing cards and smoking cigarettes with any number of her siblings who lived as houseguests at my expense. It was nice, for a change, to be able to have an intelligent conversation with someone. Talking to Mary was like trying to have a conversation with a Corona bottle.

26
Charlie

In 1972 I met *Charlie*. Her real name was Sharon and a friend of hers was Paul Vino. Cocaine was the drug of choice for the hip people. She lived in Oakland at the time when I met her. I also met this white boy named Budd, who was an attorney. He was new to California, and seemed very cool. He became the attorney for the Natural Four and I thought we would become good friends. I soon found out this was not going to be the case. I went to his office for the first time and there was this red-headed lady working for him. I was attracted to her but nothing happened between us, although I could tell she liked me too. *Charlie* smiled very happily, in Budd's office, when she saw me, and I responded the same to her.

One day I went to Budd's office to sign some papers. He was not in yet so I sat down and started talking to *Charlie*. I could see she was not her normal self, so I asked her what was the problem and she began to cry. I tried to console her. She began to tell me what was wrong. She told me her boyfriend was on drugs, had stolen a lot of items from her house, and that she did not know what to do. I said "Maybe he will change" and held her. She stopped crying. About a week later I went back to the office and she was sitting in the same place. She said she had put him out and was feeling the blues because she cared for him. I asked if she would like to go have lunch with me, and she accepted. I told her about the problems I was having with my wife, at the time. This was before DNA testing. We became very close friends and evolved into lovers. I say this with great fondness because *Charlie* taught me what it was to make love with passion and deep feelings for your partner.

The first time we were together she held me close to her, making me feel like I was the only man in the world. It was raining heavily outside, and I went to her apartment just to smoke some weed, talk, drink some brandy and toot a little cocaine. One thing led to another and, before we knew it, we were making love, with the rain, lightning and thunder crashing. It was like nothing else I had ever experienced in my life up to that point. I was in a daze for a long time after this. I went home and could not think of anything but this beautiful women and what she had just done to me. Our relationship lasted for five long years, and we are still friends. We don't see each other very often. Every once in a while I will run into her in a restaurant, but I will never forget *Charlie*, nor how we made love that first night.

Charlie also became a benefactor for the group in a lot of ways. She helped us out, financially, on several occasions. Once, we were stuck in Atlanta with no funds to pay the band and she sent me enough money to do so and get us back home. Delmos and I got into a fight over the money she had given me. *Charlie* joined me on short trips to help plan promotions for the group, and she had a collection of the Natural Four photos, press releases, etc. This made her a tremendous asset to the group, and to me.

Delmos was locked up in Los Angeles for another liquor store robbery. None of us knew he had committed this crime. Apparently, Delmos had gone to L.A., where he and some other friends committed this holdup. We had a show in Atlanta, at a club called the Scarlet O'Hara, but Delmos was not there when it came time to perform. So, we went on without him.

After the show I spoke to Marv, our so-called manager, and told him we needed to change singers because Delmos was a problem. Leroy Hutson vetoed my decision. He was one of our main producers. Leroy was fond of Delmos and wanted to keep him around. That was another time when I lost control.

I was pretty much handling business matters for the group, taking care of such things as paying the band members as well as the principal members of the Natural Four. When Delmos showed up he fought me over my money. He thought he should get more, for some stupid reason, but I was not about to let that happen. We exchanged blows a few times over this. I took what was left of the money and left the hotel where we were staying. A friend of mine called my brother, CJ, asking him if he would ride with me back to California.

Amid the pressures of touring, I was having trouble urinating and it was getting worse each day. It would take me forever to use

97

the bathroom. My brother and I drove from Atlanta to California in two days. We stopped only to get gas and a quick bite to eat. Once we were back in California, it became more difficult for me to urinate. I had to go to the hospital where I was only able to use the bathroom with the help of a catheter. It was the most humbling experience I ever had in my life. I was told that I had a stricture and that I would need an operation immediately. It would cause me more problems later on in my life.

Charlie and I broke up when I went into the hospital in 1975 to have my operation. She came to see me once in the hospital. It was very serious and I was down for nearly three months. The Natural Four was coming to an end.

Charlie's house was destroyed and she lost all of the group memorabilia in her possession during the Oakland firestorm of 1991. She had recording demos and posters that you cannot find today. There were even buttons and little dolls made in the likenesses of the Natural Four, but all was lost in the fire.

I was out of commission for two and half months after my surgery. We were having serious problems at this point. Steve, Delmos, and Darryl wanted to replace me in the group. I wanted Delmos out but Steve and Darryl wanted to keep him in the group. So, they tried to go on without me. I was working with my sons, Mark and Christopher, doing commercials. Mark was doing quite well as a child actor, so things were good in that department. The Natural Four tried to carry on, performing two or three shows without me, but with little success. I was not surprised because there was no longer any leader. I was out, Delmos was doing his usual criminal acts, and Steve and Darryl were just trying to maintain.

Tensions between Delmos and I were high. To show what kind of a person Delmos is, after I had moved to LA, and lived there for a few years, I went back to Oakland to visit friends and such. Delmos' dad had an auto repair shop in West Oakland, so I thought I would just stop by and say hello. His dad was working on a car when I got there, and we began to chat. As the conversation went along, and we spoke of the Natural Four, he told me a story about an incident that had happened one time when he, Delmos, and his brother, Robert, went fishing in the San Francisco Bay. He said that they were drinking beer and, as time passed, Delmos got really drunk and started to say a lot of crazy things. According to Mr. Whitley, Delmos knew that his dad could not swim when they got into a heated argument. Delmos threatened to throw his father overboard. If it weren't for his other son, Robert, he said. he is sure Delmos would have done just as he said he was going to do. I believed him, because I have been around Delmos when he was intoxicated.

Mr. Whitley's story made me remember a time when we were touring in Texas, and at a hotel swimming pool. Our guitar player, Greg Crocket, could not swim and Delmos kept saying to him, "Come on in, man. I will catch you." Greg jumped in and, of course, Delmos moved out of the way. Steve had to swim over to Greg and save him while Delmos laughed at him. Mr. Whitley also told me, unforgettably, that he believes the Natural Four broke up because of Delmos. It's not something I didn't already know, but it was good to have my opinion confirmed by a third party.

27
Pasadena

I was working with Mark and Christopher in Los Angeles, doing television commercials and shows. After my hospital stay in 1975-'76, I decided to move there to improve the boys' chances of working. Mark and I headed south in '77, leaving Christopher, Monique and Mary in the Bay Area until we were settled in.

Mark and I moved into a hotel near Hollywood and stayed there for about six months, going out on interviews and "cattle calls." All aspiring actors have to go through this process when trying to break into the Hollywood scene. We were able to live okay because of the commercials Mark booked. They paid well-enough for us to maintain the hotel room. I went back to the Bay Area, sold my house, and moved the whole family to Pasadena. I managed to get a job at J.C. Penney's and delivered newspapers seven days a week. Mary found work as a nurse's aide in a local convalescent hospital in Pasadena. It was an up-scale hospital that catered to movie stars like Tony Curtis. Things were going well. Our house was on Howard Street. During this time, I came face to face with The John Birch Society.

We initially settled in South Pasadena. After living there for only a month, pamphlets were placed on our front door on Saturday mornings, with messages like, "Get Rid of Niggers, Jews, and Mexicans from California." One Saturday, I waited for them to come up to my door. As they were ready to put that trash underneath my door, I opened it and there stood three old, white ladies. You can imagine their shock once they saw I was Black. Not only did we have problems with this kind of thing, but I was also getting problems from Mark's school, Marengo Elementary. Mark had done several episodes of *Eight is Enough,* in which he played a friend of the kid character named Nicholas, and all of Mark's classmates knew him from the show. He was also easy to remember as the only Black kid in the classroom.

The children were not the problem; it was his teacher, Mr. Johnson. Mark was voted in as president of his class, over another kid that was the teacher's pet. Mark's achievement didn't sit well with Mr. Johnson. So, I went up to the school and confronted him, which did not sit well with the entire school. Mark never had his meeting as class president, even though he was the grand marshal for the annual South Pasadena parade. Traditionally, these kinds of parades used locally-owned, vintage cars to carry the grand marshal, but this particular year all those cars were cancelled. They had to use cars from Los Angeles for the parade that year.

Music never stopped in the Bell-James household. I kept on working with Mark and Christopher, and sometimes with Monique. I started an acting class with young kids, working with them on their vocals. I also continued to deliver papers seven days a week. Mary started having an affair with the son of the owner of a real estate company. I didn't see it happening; I was working the paper route and Mary was supposedly busy between the convalescent hospital and working part-time at the real estate office. Her comings and goings were strange. At first I did not think anything about it because we were supposed to be saving money to get ahead. If she was working extra hours then that was a positive. But she never brought any money home and she was gone for days at a time.

I kept right on working with my sons, trying to keep music happening, and commercials coming in. I started a new band in Pasadena, with Mark on piano and Christopher singing lead. I even tried to get Monique involved, for a short period of time. Mary, by then, had become very bold. She would have this guy she was seeing drop her off at the house. She didn't care whether or not I saw him. We were operating at the height of marital dysfunction.

As Mary was out enjoying her dalliances, I maintained my focus on the boys, working with them to get more commercial work. There was even a time when Christopher tried-out for a Bill Cosby Jell-O commercial. This is when I became acquainted with how fucked-up Bill Cosby was. Christopher went into the casting room while I stood by the door. I heard Cosby yell at the casting director, "I don't want no more niggers on the commercial. Get him out of here." I was shocked and so very angry. I could not believe he said that, about a child, no less.

28
Christopher Paul

My son, Christopher was born in 1973. I had turned 30 that year and things were going well with the Natural Four. The Natural Four was the big thing in the Bay Area at the time. I will never forget picking him up from the hospital and bringing him home. I was one very proud father. Christopher was the only child that I was in some way prepared to deal with, as a real father.

Monique was in my life before I knew what was happening, and then Mark came 11 months after. Before, there had been no time for me to understand what being a father meant. In 1965, fresh out of the service, my life as I knew it was over. With Christopher it was 10 years later and much different. I walked around the neighborhood, showing him off to some friends of mine. We were living on 54th Street. He was a beautiful baby, and by this time my thoughts of Margaret were a distant memory. All I could think of was my music and my new son.

As Christopher grew older I could see he was as talented as Mark. The Natural Four were doing a lot of shows and traveling, so I was in and out, but I did spend a lot of time with all three of the children. As Christopher became more and more musically-inclined I knew he was going to be a star. Or, at least, this was my hope. Now, on the other hand, Christopher was also a very mischievous child, even at a young age, but I never thought anything of it.

Christopher's interest in music grew with the passing of time. He sang with Mark and me. He was very young, maybe three or four, but even at that tender age he could hold his own when it came to harmonies. Christopher picked it up so quickly. I was surprised and very happy. When he was five or six years old I began taking Christopher with me when Mark had auditions and "cattle calls." "Cattle calls" are sessions when many children are called to try-out, to be cast for commercials and small parts in TV shows. Christopher would come along and want to get involved. For a long time I would not let him because he was not in the union. One day I took him along to a "cattle call" for a water park commercial. At this audition there were quite a lot of children playing, and, naturally,

Christopher wanted to play. I kept holding him back, but one of the assistant directors saw Christopher trying to play with the other children and said, "Let him go play." I said, "But he is not in the union." And she replied, "Don't worry, we can make that happen." That was the start of Christopher doing television commercials. He did several more after that. He was good, but he was also very stubborn and wanted to do things his own way. Unlike Mark, Christopher was very head-strong. Soon I would see just how head-strong he was.

The Natural Four was still gigging while Christopher and Mark were still auditioning. This went on for another couple of years. The Natural Four broke up in 1975-76. My sons and I had moved to Los Angeles to further their careers. However, prior to leaving the Bay Area, I formed another band called Saint James Version, consisting of me, Mark and Christopher. We were very good and Christopher was a standout singer. We performed a few shows in and around San Francisco and the Bay Area which were quite successful, but there was only one problem: Christopher would not focus. During a show in San Francisco the audience threw money on the floor and Christopher stopped singing to pick it up, even though I told him not to. The first time I recorded in a studio with Christopher and Mark I knew what a gifted singer Christopher was. We recorded several songs: The two I remember the most were "Be by Your Side" and "Father and Son."

We played the Playboy Club in L.A., and they loved Christopher. There was one time when they were preparing to film the sequel to the movie *Roots*. Christopher went out for the audition. I worked really hard to get him ready for this; it would have made him a star. I was certain he would get the part because they called him back several times. He did not get it and I was very disappointed, wondering why, even though I knew deep inside it was because of his stubborn attitude. The casting director was Rubin Cannon, a very famous casting director and a Black man. After my second or third time asking, I was told by Mr. Cannon's assistant that he loved Christopher but that he would not follow directions. Christopher would not keep to the script and that would not work. I didn't know then that this would lead to a long period of problems I would have with Christopher.

After six years in Pasadena and going through the crazy changes with Mary, I decided to move back to the Bay Area. I was still dealing with Budd, who was handling both of the boys' money from their TV shows and commercials. So, I sent Mary ahead to find us an apartment or a house to live in. She had to get the funds from Budd, which turned out to be a big mistake on my part. The house she picked in Oakland was a rat-infested, roach haven; a run-down, unclean, shack on a street named Nicole. My brothers, Albert and CJ helped me repair and clean up the house so we could move in. Oh my God; I could not believe she would do this or that Budd would let her get this rat- infested house for our family. We lived there for about a year and a half. Mary went back to work for the convalescent hospital she had worked in before our move to L.A.

Christopher started going to Bret Harte Middle School, in Oakland, CA. I went to work selling computers for Computer Craft in San Francisco. It was about this time that Christopher started to get into real trouble. He started cutting school and hanging out with the wrong group of people. He was around 10 or 11 and I was thinking Mary was handling things with Christopher because she was on that side of the bay in the daytime, and I was working in San Francisco. Again, I was not using my head and still thinking Mary would do what most mothers do when it comes to their children, especially their youngest child. I am not saying that I should not have done a better job. I know I could have, in many ways, but hindsight, as they say, is 20/20 vision.

We moved to Coolidge Street in 1985. This is where things got real rough for Christopher. Mary and I were not getting along. She would take trips back to Los Angeles to see the guy she was seeing before we left Pasadena. I was trying to make ends meet, and trying to keep the family together. Because I was caught up in my own personal world, during this time, Christopher was able to run amok. So I have to take some of the blame for myself.

Christopher was skipping school because neither his mother nor his father was paying attention. Even though he was staying with us, she was too busy working and taking care of Budd's children, instead of her own child. Christopher started to do his own thing. It went from bad to worse.

The first time he went to jail, which was in Oakland, I was called to get him out. I don't remember what he was in jail for doing, but it did not matter. He was my son and I know I should have been more on top of things. He was living with his mother because I was not stable in my living situation at the time. I did not feel it was a good idea to take him from school to school while I was trying to get my own life together. I felt that since Mary had a solid job and was still living in the Coolidge house, it was better for him to live with her.

Christopher became increasingly rebellious, acting out more and more. When he was about fourteen I suggested he come and live with me. Christopher did not want to hear this and I did not want to seem like the bad guy forcing him to come and stay with me. That was the wrong thing to do. There were times when he was skipping school and I would go looking for him. His mother and I were not speaking at all. This left Christopher to his own devices, and that meant he was going to get into more trouble, especially in Oakland at that time.

Christopher went to prison while he was staying with his mother, and I was not in the loop at all. What makes things even worse for me, personally, is that Delmos, the one member that caused the most problems in the Natural Four, was in touch with Christopher while he was in prison. It was like punishment for me to hear these things. I went to see Christopher several times in prison, and each time it was as though I was dying inside. At first I had abandoned my oldest son, and now I was losing my youngest son to the system.

29
Maya: My Daughter

Remember that long tour that Paula the ice skater took? She was giving birth to our daughter, and giving her up to a family. However, more than 20 years passed before I knew that Maya existed. I never had a clue that Paula bore my child, even though we continued to see each other for years. She called me often and I also spoke to her mother, but neither said a word. I now know that her mother was also unaware, at least that's what I have been led to believe. How Paula kept this secret all this time still keeps me guessing. I remember when and how I first found out about Maya. I had been with my second wife, Zakiya, for several years, and had told her about most of my life and other relationships I had been in. When I talked to her about Paula, it was always with fond memories, so it was a shock to find out about Maya, in the way I did.

Paula called one day, inviting Zakiya and me to her wedding. I was thrilled at the invite. Paula said she was in a relationship and very happy. I was glad for her. Time passed, maybe fifteen months or so, before I got a call from her saying she was having problems with her husband and needed to talk. I told her "anything I can do," but that it would be difficult for me to be objective under the circumstances. I knew she understood, but she called back a few times to tell me things were getting worse and she did not know what to do. More time passed and she called back again, this time talking to Zakiya. When I returned, Zakiya told me Paula called for me once again. About two days later, I got another call from her and this time she sounded very upset, saying she needed to talk to me right away. I began to question her intentions.

Paula said she wanted to meet me somewhere, so I said "Okay, but in a public place." Some of the possibilities racing through my mind were scary. I dreamed up a scenario that she was setting me up like O.J. Simpson: a situation where she kills her husband and makes me the fall guy. So we met at a McDonald's in San Mateo. I arrived before her and waited to see exactly what was up. It didn't help my nerves when she pulled up in a Bronco.

"Funny," I said to myself. She got out of the SUV with her mother and I could see there was no one else with them. I called out to them and she motioned for me to come and get in her vehicle. Once I got into the car she blurted out "You have a daughter." I replied, "Yes," thinking of Monique. Paula responded, "No, you have a daughter named Maya and here is her number. I don't want to have anything else to do with her." I was in shock! I told her I couldn't understand why she did not tell me this before, years ago, and asked what happened to make her tell me now. She told me she was trying to protect me and did not want to disrupt my marriage. I explained to her that she should have given me the opportunity to decide on my own and not take that choice away from me. I had already lost Johnny, my first son with Margaret, and now I was losing another child because of the actions of others. I was not happy at all about this and I let her know that. The last time I spoke to Paula was about a week or two after she had laid that trip on me.

I called Maya and invited her to my house. She was overcome with emotion and began to cry. We set it up for her to come over about a week later. When we first met, it was wonderful. Our physical resemblance made it clear that she was my daughter, but we decided to take the DNA test to be sure. When it was over we knew the truth.

Our relationship went well for a couple of years. I had a great time with Ashley and Devon, my two new granddaughters. They are beautiful girls. I tried to spend as much time with Maya as she would allow me to spend with her, which wasn't much. About two years into the new father-daughter relationship, I saw a change in Maya's attitude toward me. I couldn't quite put my finger on it, but it was as though she wanted me to be like her foster father. I noticed she had a picture of him over her bed. I didn't say anything but felt this was very strange. She told me how she and her foster father would get drunk and spend a lot of time together. She also said she did not get along with her stepmother. I never asked about him, her foster father, but felt there was something not quite right with their relationship.

Maya told me about her marriages and how she fought with her husbands, quite violently. She told me how she spit on them and

108

hit them, which was very disturbing. I felt she wanted me to be broke and have nothing, so she could take charge of my life. She did not count on me or Zakiya being as strong as we were.

We visited each other off and on when she came to my home in Tracy, California, to spend the night a few times. She and her children would also spend some time at my home in Oakland.

Maya became more confrontational with me about little things I couldn't quite put my finger on. She was always cool with Zakiya. The end came about three years into this new family, after she married someone who I never did meet. As it is, I don't know his name. She never told me. Maya's behavior struck me as impulsive, which I recognized as something she inherited from me. In any case, the end of our relationship came about in a very strange way. Maya had a fight with her new husband. I don't know the details of it, but, according to my oldest granddaughter, it was Maya's fault. I may never know what happened. She had asked me if she could stay in the house in Tracy. Since Zakiya and I were not staying there full-time, I told her of course she could stay. Reasonably-enough, I asked who would be staying with her. She has not spoken to me ever since.

My youngest son, Christopher took a trip to Sacramento to meet his half-sister for the first time. "She was really cool," he said, and as soon as he saw her he knew she was his sister. He was surprised that she was bi-racial. He knew about his half-German brother, but he didn't know I was into white women to the degree that I was.

30
My Son Mark

I first noticed Mark's talent when he was five years old. He would sit in on Natural Four rehearsals as we ran through our choreography, using pencils as drumsticks and my grandmother's old stool as his drum. When he got home from school, if we were practicing, he got his sticks and played the stool. He was quite good. I decided to buy him a drum kit to see what would happen. As I suspected, he was a natural. Before he started to play drums, I also noticed that he could dance very well. He was as good as Michael Jackson. On several occasions, I took Mark to the clubs with me and he was so good that I let him dance on top of the tables. He danced at one club in particular, the Showcase, located on Grove Street (now Martin Luther King Jr. Boulevard). Children were not allowed in bars, but we were The Natural Four. The club owner, Don Barksdale, was a friend of mine, and one of the first Black basketball players in the NBA. He played for the Boston Celtics during the 1950s.

I saw that Mark was endowed with many talents, so I asked him to choreograph steps for the group. He frequently accompanied me on road trips with the Natural Four. I wanted him to get a feel for life in the world of entertainment. I pushed him harder, not so hard that it would damage him, but hard enough to make him one of the best. I could see, in him, a star just like M.J.. I thought this would be great for him, and for our family as a whole. The Natural Four's attorney, Budd, took note of Mark's talent and asked to manage him, so I said agreed. I secured most of Mark's gigs, such as his first local television show *Just Kidding*. He was a weekly artist on the show. I am not sure how exactly Mark landed the show, but it was the shape of things to come.

This little, fair-skinned Black kid with an *Afro* could dance and sing like an old pro. I knew he could sing because I taught him everything I knew about vocal harmonies. He joined the actors' union and became successful starring in commercials. One of his biggest commercials was a campaign for M&M's candy.

Mark would land principal roles in the commercials because of the work we put in. I worked with Mark, preparing him for how to look into the camera, how to smile, and to always be ready to have your picture taken. He was an excellent student. Mark went on to do cereal commercials, theme-park commercials, drug abuse ads, and many others. Mark also learned how to tap dance from the legendary Fayard Nicolas, of the famed Nicholas Brothers. Mark studied with him for about two and a half years. Needless to say, he became an excellent tap-dancer.

Mark traveled with us to Denver, New York, St. Louis, and Chicago as the opening act for the Natural Four. In Denver, we were working at a club called the Shapes. The owner's name was Eugene, and he ran the club with his brothers. They were involved in the drug trade. Some of those drug deals were also made at my home in Oakland, in my kitchen. One night at the Shapes our drummer quit, so Mark had to play the Natural Four shows. He was about eight or nine at the time. He had his own tiny drum set and he held down the groove. He was always very good, so good that Eugene gave Mark his own paycheck at the end of the show, making sure my son got all of it. Mark, naturally, gave the money to his mother. From there, it never went into the family budget.

Mark played parts in television shows, "Movie of the Week" and "After-School" special programs. One of his bigger roles was playing Jackson on the hit television series *Eight Is Enough*. The Natural Four was still active and Mark was doing very well. Mary loved this very much because I was always busy doing other things, so I did not have time to observe her mischief. She was having a good time sleeping with whomever she wanted to and so was I. We were the perfect Black Hollywood couple, replete with dysfunction. By this time, we had moved to L.A. and lived in South Pasadena for a year and a half.

We saw, first-hand, how Hollywood was, for real, in the 70's. One day, while on set, Mark came to me and asked why his television mother was a maid on the show *Eight Is Enough*. I tried to explain that it was just a TV show, and nothing more, but he was adamant about the point. Like a good father, I asked the writers the same question. Afterwards, they changed the mother's part from

111

maid to secretary. All seemed well, until the next episode when they wrote Mark out of the script. It was among the coldest things I had ever seen in my life. We finished that day's shooting and everyone was smiling and kissing and hugging, so we went home feeling good. But, the next morning when we arrived at the set, they had a table for us, and a table for them, *them* being all of the white people and the "Uncle Toms" who worked with them. They turned their backs on us, as if we did not exist. They let him finish out the week, but they did not talk to us, or even look at us, for that matter. Mark did not understand, so I tried to explain the best I could, hoping he would eventually get it.

Mark booked parts on *The Love Boat, White Shadow, The Lou Grant Show*. He was thriving as a child actor, and Budd was handling all of Mark's money, as well as Mary's money. While Mary was busy doing her thing and I was busy doing mine, Budd was busy doing us.

I placed my trust in Budd, and didn't pay attention to how he was misappropriating our money. It was hard enough trying to make the Natural Four and my family run smoothly. Mary was doing her usual, running the streets and taking care of Budd's children, not caring that she had her own children to take care of. I complained to her about this a lot, but it was a waste of time. Budd and his wife were using drugs, so Mary got mellow anytime she wanted, and she took full advantage. She would leave her job at the convalescent hospital to be home for maybe an hour before leaving to go to Budd's house. This often left Monique to take on the task of cooking for Chris, Mark and me. When Mary came home late I wasn't happy with her, but what could I say? I was in and out, myself. But I can truthfully say that I spent more time with the kids than she did.

Things came to a head in 1974-'75 with the Natural Four. We were in Chicago, doing a show with Curtis Mayfield, the Impressions, and the O'Jays at the Chicago Amphitheater. We were the opening act. Mark opened for us, tap-dancing, blowing the crowd away. When we came out, there was no proper microphone set up for us, but we played the show anyway. I was mad. When we got back-stage I went crazy on our business manager, Marv, the

Jewish boy who used us up. It was a mistake on my part, because things went south from there. We did a few more shows using Marv as our manager, but things were never the same between us. It is something I regret to this day, I should have been a lot more understanding, and approached the problem without anger or disrespect to another person!

Original Natural four

Ollan

Original
Natural Four

2nd Natural Four

Natural four
Curtom
Studio

Natural Four
Top Star Awards
Oakland, CA

Midnight Special TV Show

Chicago Gig
Steve & Ollan

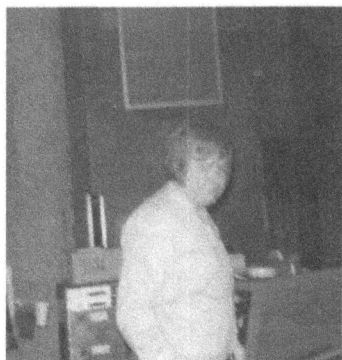

**Bob Vierra, engineer
Sierra Sound**

Birthday party for Curtis & Chris

**Friends from Boston, my birthday
party, Holiday Inn, New York, City**

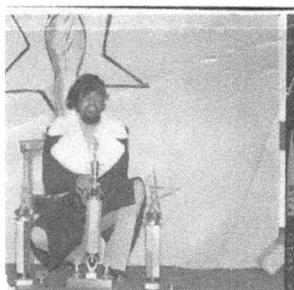

Drummer, Gaylord Birch

**Curtis Mayfield family
members at Curtom Studio**

**Lorell Simon, Songwriter
Leroy Hutson, Producer**

Berkeley Community Theater

Holiday Inn, Bud, Marv Stuart and Natural Four

At home on 54th St, Oakland, CA

Sportsman Club, Oakland, CA

Berkeley Community Theater
Oakland, CA

Top Star Awards, Lemington Hotel
Oakland, CA

Berkeley Community Theater with son Mark

Natural Four with Leroy Hutson Chicago, IL

Session, Curtom Studio Chicago, IL

Natural Four w/ Impressions

Chris w/ DJ from KDIA Radio Station

Steve & Chris Berkeley Community Theater

Sportsman Club, Grove St.,
Oakland, CA

Chris, Safari Club
San Jose, CA

Chicago, IL, record release party & show

Showcase Club
Oakland, CA

New Birth, Recording Artist
"Wild Flower"

Safari Club, San Jose, CA

Sportsman Club
Oakland, CA

Record Release Party, Chicago, IL

Promo - March of Dimes in LA, CA

31
DNA on Monique

I first heard about DNA testing in 1988. It was brand new on the public scene, so I decided that we needed to clear the matter of Monique's paternity once and for all. Joseph, Monique, and I each took the test. When the results came back, I was so far off the charts that it wasn't even a question. However, Joseph was right there up front. Mary was oblivious. Testing was new and not proven enough to make it real, as far as she was concerned. She called the results "Bullshit" and said it didn't prove anything. We all knew that it was the only thing that proved who is lying and who is not.

Mary and I discussed the whole situation, and she asserted that I did not know what I was talking about. We yelled at each other, and Mary screamed as though I had hit her, something I never did in our entire marriage, even though she hit me on several occasions. Mark was home at the time and thought I had done something to his mother, so he came running into the room screaming at me, saying he was going to take Christopher and leave. He saw that I had not put my hands on his mother, but things were never the same between us, afterwards. To this day, Mary maintains DNA testing is not accurate science and that Monique is my child, by blood and birth.

Monique & Joseph's
DNA Test Results 1988

INSTITUTE OF FORENSIC SCIENCES
CRIMINALISTICS LABORATORY

2945 WEBSTER STREET, OAKLAND, CALIFORNIA 94609
Telephone: (415) 451-0767

AUGUST 12, 1988

CHARLES V. MORTON, *Director*

PATERNITY BLOOD TEST — IFS/CL# C-88315

SYSTEM	ALLEGED FATHER OLLAN BELL-JAMES	ALLEGED FATHER JOSEPH BELL	MOTHER MARY JAMES	CHILD MONIQUE JAMES JOHNSON
ABO	0	0	A1	0
MN	MN	MN	MN	N
Rh	ce	cDe	CcDe	CcDe
EsD	1	1	1	1
PGM	1+	1+1-	2+1+	2+1+
GLO1	2-1	1	2-1	2-1
EAP	B	BA	BA	BA
ADA	1	1	1	1
AK	1	1	1	1
Hp	1	2	1	2-1
Gc	1	1	1	1
Tf	C	C	C	C
PepA	1	1	1	1
CA II	1	1	1	1

CONCLUSIONS: Based on these results, Ollan Bell-James is not the biological father of Monique James Johnson. The Hp system provides a first-order exclusion of paternity. The child possesses the "2" gene which is not present in the mother's specimen. Therefore, the child must have inherited the "2" gene from her biological father. Since Ollan Bell-James lacks this gene, he cannot pass it to offspring, and is therefore excluded from paternity.

Joseph Bell cannot be excluded as being the biological father of Monique James Johnson. He is approximately 3.6 times as likely to pass the required paternal genes as a random black man. Assuming a prior probability of 0.5, (50%), the estimated "plausibility of paternity" is 0.7826, (78.26%), "inconclusive".

Gary A. Sims
Forensic Scientist

121

Monique's First Husband Harry

When I first met Harry I did not like him, because there was a dark cloud around him. But Monique seemed happy and I loved her so much that I decided to let her do as she pleased, even though I did not have a choice in the matter. They got married; I gave her away even though I didn't feel this man was right for my niece, my daughter! I didn't have to be a spiritual "reader" to see this. Harry was a dark spirit. He came to stay at my house when I lived on Coolidge, in Oakland. I told him that was fine, so long as he and Monique did not have sex, especially since I had younger, impressionable children in the house. Stupid me! They knew more than I did about sex and sleeping together!

Several years passed and Monique was in love with this serial rapist, but I was oblivious at the time. He had been a standout college athlete in Texas and yet couldn't find his way onto any pro football team's roster, as good as he was. I later discovered that coaches and scouts were aware of Harry's sordid history. He was, as I said before, a serial rapist, targeting Latina women. He got kicked out of school over this, although that was hardly a deterrent. He continued raping women for many more years after that.

Harry moved to the Bay Area and continued his crime spree, sometimes even with his daughter in the same room. When he was finally caught in Oakland years later it was for a low level crime. Monique called me because she was with him when he was arrested. Monique was also taken into custody and needed me to come and take Racquel, the baby, with me. Harry moved back to Texas and was eventually caught and convicted for rape. More than 15 years of raping Hispanic women. I feel these women look at all Black men as rapists. How sad is that?

It is strange how things worked out. Monique was in Texas with Harry when she saw on television that her Uncle Ray had been killed, execution style, and left on the side of the road.

Monique's Second Husband Gary Payton

Monique married Gary Payton, the NBA player, and, just like her first marriage, this was a mistake. Gary was a loud-mouthed person, with nothing that seemed like class. I will never forget Monique's wedding day. I walked her down the aisle; she was a beautiful bride, but Gary was his usual loud self. After they exchanged their wedding vows and they were walking down the aisle, a few young ladies called out to Gary, saying, "We love you!" Instead of being a stand-up guy on his and Monique's wedding day, he screamed back to this one young lady, "Just make sure you leave me your phone number!" I knew at that moment that this union wasn't going to last. He was also physically abusive to Monique. Even though she never said anything about it, I heard rumors and wouldn't see her for days at a time. The marriage lasted longer than I expected because of the kind of person Monique is. She tried in earnest to make her marriage work, no matter what. It was common knowledge that Gary was always in the streets with other women.

Years passed and things didn't change much for Monique. She stayed with Gary, even though she knew he was seeing other women. She stayed for the same reason I stayed with Mary; for the sake of the children. That was a big mistake. There was a party at the house one night and some guns were brought into the picture. My son, Mark was not speaking to me, because he favored his mother. He didn't want to hear that his mother had slept with my brother and that his sister is, in fact, his cousin. This made everyone mad at me because I was telling the truth, even if it made his mother look like a tramp.

Monique and Gary got into an argument and I'm not sure what it was about. Mark was there with his wife and children. I was told that Mark had a gun in the trunk of his car. He approached Gary, telling him that the fighting between him and his sister was not cool, and that he was going to leave, taking the children. Gary assumed Mark was going to his car to get the gun, so Gary retrieved his gun. The situation could have caused family members to die. Gary pointed his gun at Mark, who had some choice words for him. Mark told the family to leave and that was the end of the story, or so you would think.

Mark decided to sue Gary about a year later. Gary was still playing in the NBA, so Mark's lawsuit threatened to create a public relations catastrophe for him. Mark and his wife Stephanie said they were traumatized by the event, so they filed a civil suit against Gary. Gary couldn't afford this kind of press as his career in the NBA was already on the decline. He ultimately settled the matter for an undisclosed amount. Unfortunately, Mark and Stephanie did not take into consideration how their actions would affect Monique, since she was still married to this clown and he was likely going to hold her responsible for their actions.

This whole episode dragged on for years and I was dragged into it. I was accused of urging Mark to file suit against Gary, when I didn't have any idea that any of this was going on. I was getting my information second-hand. I was not part of the inner circle, because I had left Mark's mother, so he was not concerned about me whatsoever. It did not matter what his mother had done; I was the bad guy because she could do no wrong. I learned to live with this kind of thing, by staying to myself and trying to do my music. I prayed that I would make it out of this lifestyle in one piece. Mark and I have never mended our relationship. He has chosen another person to look at as his father. Of course it hurts, but what can I say?

32
Meeting Zakiya

The first time I met Zakiya was not long after my mother passed away. It was at Club Martinique, in Oakland, California. I was out with my oldest sister, Lynne. We had been dancing. She was a very good dancer and so was I. I was thinking about what I should do with my life since I had been waylaid by the news that my daughter, Monique, was, in fact, my brother's child.

Lynne and I went into the bar to have a drink. We were there about an hour when this lady came in, and there was only one seat left. Zakiya was not like anyone I was typically interested in. She was just another sister. I motioned to her, letting her know there was one empty seat next to me. She came over and sat down. A few seconds later brothers came out the woodwork, asking her to dance. She was interested in some guy sitting on the other side of her. That was cool with me, because I was looking for a different type of woman, anyway. Nevertheless, she turned back to me and we started talking. She told me her name was Zakiya, and I told her mine. A song came on the jukebox and there was no one else to dance with. My sister was at the bar. She had a serious drinking problem and didn't look like she was in any condition to dance, so I asked Zakiya if she would like to dance. She said "Yes," so we danced and talked, becoming more familiar with each other. As the evening progressed, I asked her the usual questions like "Do you have a family?" and "Where do you work?" That's when she told me her father was John Lee Hooker. I had worked with John Lee Hooker years before, in Berkeley, California, so I knew him quite well. There was a club called the Keystone, on University Avenue, where we performed together, as well as the Berkeley Community Theater, still a wonderful place for shows.

Zakiya and I talked, and, for some reason, I asked her if she could cook. I don't know why that question came to me, except that I had been eating Mary's horrible cooking for over 20 years, and I needed some relief! So, I felt I had nothing to lose if she could not cook a good meal. Her answer was straight to the point. "Of course,

I can cook. I have three boys and my ex-husband was a chef." The next thing out of my mouth was "Will you cook for me?" She laughed, saying "Sure, I'll cook for you." The evening went on and we danced a couple more times. This one guy kept on bothering her to the point when she had to be real rude to him. She cut him down to size, and soon afterward he left the club. I was taken aback by the way she got him out of her face. I laughed because it was not pretty.

I got up to go the bathroom, but when I returned Zakiya was gone. I ran out of the front door just as she was getting into her car, yelling very loudly, "Hey, I thought you said you were going to cook me a meal!" She laughed and I ran across the street, but before she could pull off I gave her my menu request: fried chicken, greens, corn bread, candied yams, and macaroni and cheese. This was not at all normal behavior for me. I reassured her, "I am not some crazy man, looking to hurt you. I don't carry a gun and I'm not an abuser. All I want is a good meal." Like I said before, after eating Mary's nasty food for 20-plus years, what did I have to lose? So, she gave me her address and we became friends from that point on. She told me to come to her house on Sunday afternoon, around three. I was there on the dot. It was one of the best meals I had eaten in a long time. From that day on we have been working together on several different projects, such as selling computers to churches and pursuing our musical passions. Again, music has saved my life and helped me through very bad times.

33

A Letter to My Son Johnny

My Dear Son, Johnny,

In a man's life he makes many mistakes: some small, some large, and some without words to describe the enormity of the mistake. I made the greatest mistake of all: I allowed someone else to control my life, and, in doing so, gave up a man's greatest gift. That gift is watching his first-born child grow up. Watching when he learned how to talk, how to walk, how to ride a bike and how to play ball. I lost seeing you cry and wiping away your tears. I missed helping you with your homework and scolding you if you didn't study. I missed kissing you when you did good, and holding you when you were not feeling well. I missed reading you to sleep, so you would not be afraid of the dark. I missed your first date, and teaching you how to drive, and all the things that a father is supposed to do when he is blessed to have a healthy son. I let other people tell me what to do and how I should do it. I was not a man; I was a boy. And, for this, I lost everything.

I have no words to talk about my lack of education, my lack of strength, my fear of my mother, your grandmother, nor my fear of Mary and her manipulating family. I have no excuses for failing to stand up for what was right and not fighting back, except that I was afraid. Fear is not an excuse, but is the truth. I was a man in name only, because a real man would have told his mother to go to hell and found a way to get back to Germany, to take care of his first born and the woman he loved.

To say I am sorry would be less than nothing, so I will not say that. To say I am ashamed is more to the truth, because I feel deep shame for what I let happen to you and your mother. I let my mother and my ex-wife make your mother and your grandmother suffer. I will take this to my grave, and, just like you and your mother suffered, I will suffer too because I don't have you and my grandchildren in my life. What a price to pay for not standing up and being a man. Johnny, please forgive me.

If you can find it in your heart, that would be enough for me to leave this world, knowing you understand that I did not do this because I did not want you. I wanted you more than anything in the world. You were the first life I helped to create. I talked to you when you were in your mother's stomach. I was just lost and could not find a way out of that moment.

Please forgive me for not being a man. I will close by saying that, if it is any consolation to you, I am an empty person, even with three other children that are my own. I find no peace, because we very rarely talk. Your youngest brother has his problems, and doesn't speak to me. Your sister, Maya, will also not speak to me, for whatever reason. I don't know about your other brother, Mark; he is just lost to me. Am I happy? There are times when I am calm, when I am around good people. Johnny, I cannot take my mind off of you and how I let you grow up without me in your life. And, I've become sad, very sad. So, I ask again, would you please, please forgive me?

Johnny

Christopher Paul

Mark Anthony

Maya with my grandaughters
Ashley & Devon

All My Children

In Closing

What Happened To the Natural Four?

the (Original) Natural Four (1st Group)

Chris James/Ollan Bell: Living in Atlanta and still singing. I am the Owner/Operator of Boom Boom Recording Studio, doing recording, engineering and production. I am producing Zakiya Hooker and I produced *"Face to Face" 2002 on* John Lee Hooker. I perform regularly in Argentina and in Europe.

John January is now retired, and living in Arizona.

Alfred Milton "Punkin" Bowden is a minister.

Allen Richardson is a retired Longshoreman.

The Natural Four (2nd Group)

Steve Striplin passed away in 2005, at 60 years old.

Darryl Canady is deeply religious. He has no more affiliation with R&B/Soul music.

Delmos Whitley is currently serving a prison sentence in a California State Prison. He is the primary reason for the breakup of the Natural Four.

EPILOGUE

Mary and I were not together. She was living in one place and I another, and there was no love lost between us. During the time we were estranged I received the bad news that Mary had cut up all my Natural Four stage clothes, and cut me out of all the pictures of her and me. The worst part was destroying my stage clothing and pictures, memorabilia that could not be replaced.

Christopher was the one to suffer the most in the middle of all of this family turmoil and our ultimate break-up. He got a 13 year-old girl pregnant when he was just 14. This was going to be a problem. I was called to Mary's house to sit and talk with Christopher and the girl. I recommended that she have an abortion; I thought they were too young and irresponsible to have a baby. Mary and the young lady's mother overruled my opinion. Once more, I was the bad guy for suggesting abortion. Today, my grandson Christopher Jr. will not speak to me, even though we spent lots of quality time together when he was young.

I thought I was finished with all of those people who caused me so much pain and heartache throughout my life. They were out of my life, I assumed, for good. But when you have children together that never happens, and they are with us until the day we leave this planet. My life with Zakiya is exciting. We have been happy making music. We traveled all over the world, moved to Atlanta, and I spend months in Argentina doing what I love to do, singing and producing shows there. Then, out of nowhere, came a serious problem with my youngest son, Christopher, who was living in Seattle, Washington, at the time. Christopher never called me, and I was fine with that. Then I get the bad news about him through his sister, Monique.

Once back in Atlanta, after a great trip, a call came from Monique saying that Christopher had been stabbed in Las Vegas, at a Lil' Wayne concert, and was there in a hospital Intensive Care Unit. It had been over five years since I had heard from Christopher. I wanted to know how he was doing and they told me that they were not sure, but would keep me posted.

Two days later I was told that they were operating on him. I was very concerned. Several more days passed and I received another call from Monique saying that he was no longer there. Instead, he was in a Holiday Inn because he did not have insurance and they had kicked him out of the hospital.

His mother lives six hours away from Las Vegas and she was there with him, along with Monique. I asked how he was doing and they said he was in pain but okay. I asked why he was not at Monique's home. I was told he could not stay in her home because he and Gary had gotten into a dispute when Christopher had stolen something from Gary. He could not stay in the hospital, and he could not stay at Monique's. I thought "Okay, Mary can take him to her house," which was only a six hours away. I went into shock when I was told they were going to put him on a train and send him to me. I said they couldn't do that because his stab-wound seemed too serious. Immediately, I said would come get him myself, and Zakiya said the same thing. As a matter of fact, Zakiya insisted I go right away, so I did. I got on the plane, flew to Las Vegas, rented a car, and drove him 3000 miles back to Atlanta.

While on this trip, that should never have happened in the first place, Christopher almost died several times. As soon as we got to Douglasville, Ga., the very next day, Zakiya came outside and said "We need to take Christopher to the doctor," because his wound was bleeding. They had to give him an emergency operation to clean out bone chips from his wound, otherwise he would have surely died.

My question is: What kind of mother would not take her own son to her home at a time like that? She was six hours away and I was 3000 miles away. When I asked her about it her comment was "I did not think about it." That says it all.

Acknowledgement

I would like to thank a few very important people for helping me with this project: Dr. James Smith, Psychiatrist, SF, CA, for setting me on the path to healing by encouraging me to put my thoughts on paper, Christopher Patton, Owner, Blue Groove Productions, for keeping me motivated and taking my words from cassette to hard copy and starting me on this journey, Tanisha Jackson, Attorney at Law, for organizing and shaping my book. Thank you, Tanisha, for all your invaluable help and historical information, Brooklyn Born, Writer, for putting this collage together in book form, Carole Ward Allen, CEO, CWA Partners LLC, for her help editing and constant encouragement. Thank you, Rand Crook, Director/Producer with Pacific Rim Media, for his tireless work as copy editor, shepherding this manuscript, and for pushing me to be a better first-time author. Special thanks to Zakiya Hooker-Bell, my dear wife and acclaimed musician, in her own right, for her beautiful cover design, late night hours on Adobe Photoshop and MS Word, and for her steadfast support and belief in me. Last but not least Ricky LeBlanc Sr. who has proven to be a good friend and historian. Thank you all. I could not have done this without your moral and physical support.

www.ingramcontent.com/pod-product-compliance
Lightning Source LLC
Chambersburg PA
CBHW071453070426
42452CB00039B/1191